What You Can Learn from Your Teenager

LESSONS IN PARENTING
AND PERSONAL GROWTH

Jean-Pierre Kallanian M.Ed.

Copyright © 2014 Jean-Pierre Kallanian M.Ed.
Back Cover Photo by Olivier Ouimet
All rights reserved.

ISBN: 1499205899
ISBN 13: 9781499205893
Library of Congress Control Number: 2014907415
CreateSpace Independent Publishing Platform
North Charleston, South Carolina

*To Julian and Stefan for teaching me to explore,
play, inspire, and connect.*

Contents

**Introduction: Learning and Gaining Wisdom from
Your Teenager**.. ix
    An Alternative View on Parenting and Personal Growth ix
    Perception Is Everything x
    You and Your Teen Hold the Key xiii
    Clarifications xiv
    Value Your Teenager's Energy, and Embrace the
    Teen Spirit.. xv

Lesson 1: Satisfying Basic Needs 1
    Five Basic Needs 1
    Teen Dilemmas 6
    Parent Dilemmas.. 12
    Exchanging the Baton 15
    What You Can Learn from Understanding Your
    Teenager's Needs... 16
    Lesson 1 Highlights 21

Lesson 2: Examining Values................................ 23
    The Value of Values.. 23
    What You Value Counts..................................... 25
    Examining Values over Time................................ 31
    Overcoming Limitations of Values 34
    What You Can Learn from Your Teenager's Values......... 35

    List of Values 39
    Lesson 2 Highlights 40

Lesson 3: EPIC Existence **42**
    How Philosophy Simplifies Parenting. 42
    Explore. 44
    Play 47
    Inspire 50
    Connect 52
    What You Can Learn from How Your Teenager
    Explores, Plays, Inspires, and Connects 55
    Lesson 3 Highlights 59

Lesson 4: Redefining Boundaries and Reconsidering Consequences **61**
    Life's a Beach 61
    Confidence and Self-Esteem 62
    Skill 62
    Physical Condition 62
    Anxiety Disguised as Defiance 63
    Tips for Setting Limits and Determining Consequences 68
    Lines Are Sometimes Meant to Be Crossed 72
    Managing Conflict When Enforcing Limits 75
    What You Can Learn from How Your
    Teenager Redefines Boundaries and Reconsiders
    Consequences. 80
    Lesson 4 Highlights 87

Lesson 5: Connecting with Your Teen **89**
    Building a Road to a Healthy Relationship. 89
    The construction of a relationship road 91

    Do Today What You Wish for Tomorrow...................92
    Giving Attention 94
    Embracing and Supporting All Aspects of Your Teenager...96
    Skills, Interests, and Resiliency........................100
    What You Can Learn from How Your
    Teenager Connects with Himself and Others.............104
    Lesson 5 Summary 109

Lesson 6: How You Communicate **111**
    Components of Communication 111
    The Impact of Technology on Communication 114
    Promoting Dialogue....................................116
    Hear What Your Teenager Has to Say....................121
    What You Can Learn from How Your
    Teenager Communicates................................ 125
    Lesson 6 Highlights 130

Lesson 7: Ensuring Health and Wellness.................. **132**
    Care for Yourself and Your Home....................... 132
    Staying Cool When You Are Feeling Hot 138
    Preconversation Questions............................. 139
    Conversation Toolbox 140
    Learning from Mistakes 143
    The Team Approach................................... 146
    What You Can Learn from How Your Teenager Ensures His
    Health and Wellness 147
    Lesson 7 Highlights 151

Lesson 8: Fear Not, Let Go, and Move On.................**153**
    Looking Back Can Help the Relationship Move Forward .. 153

Fear, Whether Real or Imagined,
Is Important to Understand 156
Letting Go for the Sake of Holding On 160
Moving On with the End Goal in Mind .161
What You Can Learn from How Your Teenager
vDoesn't Fear, Lets Go, and Moves On 164
Lesson 8 Highlights 169

Conclusion **171**
The Conflict Over Pomegranate Juice .171

Introduction:
Learning and Gaining Wisdom from Your Teenager

There is no end to education. It is not that you read a book, pass an examination, and finish with education. The whole of life, from the moment you are born to the moment you die, is a process of learning.
                                                            Jiddu Krishnamurti

Age shows wisdom, but wisdom shows no age.
                                                            Unknown

An Alternative View on Parenting and Personal Growth

Parenting is a series of mostly unpredictable interactions between child and parent intertwined with fluctuating thoughts and emotions. It is as much of an art form as a skill. Parenting is not learned overnight, nor is there a universal handbook on how to properly raise a child. Over time, the relationship unfolds with your child having as much influence on you as you have on him. Along the way, you can learn valuable parenting tips and helpful life lessons, growing and developing individually and as a family.

Parenting is a learning process that involves taking risks and making mistakes. You will make decisions and do things that seem reasonable without knowing that your actions will produce the desired result. Parenting can make you question your confidence and take you on emotional roller coaster rides. It will have you wondering what family, friends, and neighbors think of you and leave you scratching your head, wondering what could possibly happen next.

Why does the life of a teen's parent sound like the life of a teen? It is all part of the human design to teach us how to connect with one another. Teenagers will do what anyone who wants to be better understood would do. They will directly or indirectly pull you into their world. You may begin thinking, feeling, and even behaving alike. This mirroring effect is a powerful interpersonal tactic that all humans use, given our inherent need to connect with others. Your teen wants to connect with you, and overcoming challenging parenting moments necessitates this need. Where there is adversity there is opportunity, and the person to thank for all these learning possibilities is your teen!

Every life stage presents opportunities and challenges. Unfortunately, adolescence has traditionally been branded as a time of hardship. *What You Can Learn from Your Teenager: Lessons in Parenting and Personal Growth* challenges this widely held perception and inaccurate portrayal of teens. It illustrates how this phase in life is rife with possibilities for living a more fulfilling life. Your teenager is building mental, emotional, physical, spiritual, and intuitive strength, all in preparation to deal with the realities of adulthood. The book shows appreciation by acknowledging how your teen can help you become the parent you want to be and the person you truly are.

Perception Is Everything

Parenting can be challenging, and sometimes it helps to change your perspective in order to learn and grow. It is better to see the glass half full instead of half empty. There is much to gain from looking carefully at what teens are trying to accomplish through their actions. Approach your teen's questionable behavior from a supportive perspective. The impact of your response to your teen's behaviors is greater than you think.

You can project either trust and confidence or mistrust and lack of confidence onto your teen as she takes on more responsibility, becomes more self-sufficient, and discovers her true nature. Teenagers are the embodiment of learning, and as such, there is much you can relearn from them. Recall that you were once a teen. Now you are privileged to be living with one, so be mindful of this, and take advantage of the time you have left with your teen. The tips provided in this book will help you create a long-lasting relationship and allow you to tap into the wisdom your teenager possesses.

Parenting does not mean giving every ounce of energy and minute of your time to your child. Nor does it mean that you are the sole role model, teacher, and expert on life and how to navigate it. You are in the leading position, but parenting is a process through which you can learn as much about yourself as you can about your child. You will have daily opportunities to teach your child skills and life lessons; however, you can also learn from teens about how to become more in tune with them as well as how to become more in tune with yourself.

You can always learn something in a parent-child relationship as long as you keep an open mind. Avoid generalizing the teen attitude and behavior as typical. This diminishes your teen's individuality and ability to be regarded as a contributing member of the family and society. Instead, look at your teen as someone who can offer helpful insights into improving both your relationship and your life. Teens have as many unflattering stereotypes of parents as parents have of teens. If teenagers wrote books on managing their parents' emotions and actions, imagine how those titles would read!

Some general characteristics apply to teenagers, but this can also be said of other life stages, including adulthood. Teenagers are individuals whose idiosyncrasies more accurately describe their nature. These personal traits require your full understanding and appreciation. In order for you to work most effectively with yourself, you must understand, accept, and appreciate your distinct nature as well. Teens have answers you are looking for, but you must value their existence, respect their opinion, appreciate what they are trying to achieve, and listen to what they have to say.

For sixteen years, I advocated for improved services, equal rights, and the social reintegration of youth in conflict with the law. This was a group whose voices were heard little, if at all. They appreciated someone who stood up for them, supported them in their development, gave them opportunities to try new skills, and believed in them. There was no greater reward than to see a young person accepted back at home or school. I felt an immense sense of joy when a youth passed the GED, obtained a diploma, or enrolled in a college course. There was a sense of accomplishment when a youth who had previously made money illegally went to a job interview, was hired, received a paycheck, opened a bank account, and was able to lawfully support the family.

Now I am advocating for all teenagers who are mislabeled, looked upon with mistrust, or feel underappreciated by society. I am asking you to join me in this campaign, starting with the teen living under your roof. When you see your child as someone from whom you can learn, your perception and interactions will be more healthy and rewarding. You will recognize the undervalued knowledge and wisdom within your teenager and tap into your innate parenting abilities. You will gain the confidence to go deep within yourself and rediscover potential that you left behind in your young adult years.

You and Your Teen Hold the Key

Most parenting books come from scientific research and studies on adolescent development, well-known experts, mental health professionals, and brave parents writing about family triumphs. All these viewpoints add different, relevant, and valuable perspectives on the topic of parenting adolescents, but they all neglect a valuable resource on parenting and personal growth, one traditionally portrayed as the bane of parenting and the antithesis of learning: teens.

You and your teen are well versed in each other's habits, strengths, weaknesses, triggers, and routines. I have learned, professionally and personally, that most solutions to interpersonal issues are right in front of us. Finding it is a matter of looking at people for who they are, not how we think they are or would like them to be.

Practicing the techniques presented can help you create a relationship in which trust, respect, and open dialogue become the norm, regardless of what is being discussed. Look at your teenager as a whole person. Discover the potential within him. Learn and grow by doing what your teen does best: exploring, playing, inspiring others (and being inspired), and connecting with self and others.

Decisions about parenting are not made haphazardly. Be accountable, and take responsibility. Act with intention, keep an open mind, and be creative when interacting with your teen. Creativity allows you to find new ways to use what you have before you, be it a person or an object. You may teach your child a new skill, or maybe your teen will show you something learned from having watched countless YouTube videos. Imagination knows no bounds and has limitless outcomes.

Acknowledge what you already are: the expert on your teen and on yourself. Tap into the expertise within your teenager, because she also knows you as well or better than you may know yourself. How you interact with your teenager will set an example for how she should interact with others. Likewise, how you see your teen interact with the world should be an example for how you can develop as a parent and individual.

Clarifications

This book examines both processes and actions. You will need to do more than read and reflect. You will need to engage with your teen in order to build a healthy and long-lasting relationship. Use your teenager as a model. Your teen can help you rediscover forgotten truths about yourself and of life when you closed the door to your teenage years many moons ago. Sensitive topics such as death, divorce, sex, substance abuse, violence, trauma, abuse, sexual orientation, peer pressure, and teen pregnancy are not specifically addressed; but the lessons and exercises will help you gain the skills and confidence to talk about these real life issues. Seek professional assistance when issues go beyond the capacity of the book or if you are having difficulties resolving them on your own.

Throughout adolescence, many adults will leave an impression on a teen's development. I would be remiss to assume that the term *parent* refers only to a biological parent and equally as negligent to assume that the terms *teenager, teen, adolescent, child, son,* and *daughter* refer only to a biological relationship. I use words for caretakers and teens mainly in the singular. Interpret these terms in a manner that best fits your situation.

Value Your Teenager's Energy, and Embrace the Teen Spirit

The approach I encourage you to take with your teenager is similar to the philosophy of martial arts: instead of resisting the force coming at you, use the energy to your favor. By not regarding your teen's attitude and behavior as defensive or aggressive, you will learn how to better support your teen's development and reach greater heights in your own development. This approach will create a compassionate, understanding relationship that will last well beyond the adolescent years.

When you find yourself becoming emotionally entangled in your teen's thoughts, behaviors, and feelings, do not panic. This means that you are connected—maybe too much, but connected nonetheless. If you recognize when your teenager has struck a chord within you, take a step back. It is not about you. Not getting emotionally drawn in will allow you to deal with the situation more calmly and objectively. By emotionally separating yourself, you will be able to control yourself. This will allow you to better understand the need being fulfilled and what values and rules are guiding your teen's process. The secondary gain of differentiating from your teen and keeping an open mind to the nature of adolescence is that you can gain new insights and ideas from understanding your child's way of relating to the world.

As you go through life, keep the doors to your past open, regardless of its qualities. Carry some of the adolescent spirit with you into adulthood. Knowledge, abilities, and skills gained from childhood and adolescence can serve you well as an adult. The adolescent mentality—being explorative, playful, inspiring, and open to connecting—holds the keys to living a more fulfilling life. We commonly hear parents say to adolescents, "Stop acting like a child!" Why does an adolescent need to act like an adult? What makes us believe that once we become adults, we must never act like an adolescent?

Depending on the adult mind-set alone will only get you so far in life. Is it a coincidence that we place our hands on the sides of our head when we have made a mistake? What you have done most likely is limited your decision making to just your brain. Most of life's challenges are too complex to foresee a certain outcome, or they consist of too many variables for the mind to calculate. The tools needed in such situations are instinct, trust, courage, faith, risk taking, and trial and error. Fortunately for you, the person most adept in this nonlinear way of approaching life lives under your roof. Most of what your teenager is experiencing is unanticipated and consists of too many random variables for the developing mind to process. Your teen relies on an irrational and intuitive means for navigating life.

I challenge you to question whether responding to complex situations in an adult manner is always in your best interest. Sometimes taking an instinctual adolescent approach when you are faced with a dilemma that cannot be solved by a rational, mature mind may be both necessary and effective. The decisions you make in this manner may be some of the most influential and become your favorite stories to tell.

Need additional support applying what you've read? Visit whatyoucanlearn.com.

Lesson 1:
Satisfying Basic Needs

A man travels the world in search of what he needs and returns home to find it.
George Edward Moore

All you need in life is ignorance and confidence, and then success is sure.
Mark Twain

Five Basic Needs

We all have basic needs that must be met on a daily basis. Our actions are efforts to satisfy those needs as best we can. Seeing your teen's behavior in this way will make it easier for you to not take the behaviors personally and understand that her decisions are not made with the intent of making you feel a certain way. Understanding how your teen's needs are met will help you better comprehend your relationship dynamics, shedding light on where improvements can be made. As the master in satisfying needs, your teen can give you some pointers on how to better satisfy yours. The five basic needs presented in this lesson and mentioned throughout the book—Survival, Belonging, Power, Freedom, and Fun—are common among human needs theorists and particular with teens.

Survival is a vital need that does not require much elaboration. You do your best to ensure that your teen is healthy, safe, nourished, clothed, and has appropriate housing. Teenagers take on more responsibility for fulfilling this need with age. As teens begin to contribute to living costs, they learn the value of money and how essential it is to prioritize resources. They learn basic work ethics and life skills from observing you and other important adults as well as through volunteer work, internships, schoolwork, and a part-time or full-time job.

Sex and reproduction are also included in survival. Sexual identity further develops and sexual experimentation begins during the teenage years. Your teen will learn more about these topics from peers, health specialists, the media, and hopefully you. As your relationship improves, you will be better able to talk about puberty, sexual identity, sexual orientation, and the risks associated with sexual experimentation. You will also be better able to discuss the impact these real-life teen issues have.

The need to belong is evident from birth and continues through family bonds, friendships, intimate relationships, and group affiliations. As social beings, we need to feel connected to others in meaningful ways and fulfill a good part of our needs through social connections. Belonging is essential to human existence; looking at the role that peers and romantic relationships play in your teenager's life is enough to prove this point. As your teen's concept of belonging expands beyond the confines of your home, do not despair—your bond will not disappear, but it will change in form and function. If you allow it to do so, this change can bring about deeper appreciation and respect.

Until now, you have mostly fulfilled your child's need to belong, creating conditions and parameters on how it manifested. Now your teen is going out into the world to find ways to satisfy the need through friendly, virtual, and romantic relationships. Extended family relationships, such as spending time with cousins or participating in a club, sport, or other group activity, also allow your teen to fulfill the need for belonging. You are still important to your teen even though you are no longer solely responsible for meeting this need. If you have difficulty accepting this, imagine having had a parent as your only friend or social group.

It may be easier for you to understand that one person cannot satisfy all your needs than to accept that you can no longer satisfy all of your teen's needs. The unconditional love you continue to show as your teenager approaches adulthood is important as it allows your teen to freely explore and develop personal connections and a social network. Consider your teen an explorer; you become home base, providing shelter, supplies, support, encouragement, and reassurance. If you are lucky, your efforts may result in a sign of appreciation: a note, a gift, a hug, or even the words *thank you*.

Power is a misleading need. Some see it as the ability to control others while others associate it with wealth or political influence. Others say that power is the ability to do what you want when you want. All of these definitions have a common thread: power is associated with everything outside of you, factors you can influence but over which you do not have complete authority. For some, the word *power* suggests a magical ability to control that which we in fact cannot.

No matter how badly you might like a person to change (or to blame someone for your misfortune), you render yourself powerless when you do so. True power is knowing what is in your control and focusing your intentions on that. Your reaction is not the result of what your daughter did; it is your choice. Likewise, your son does not do something because you said so; he does it because he chooses to. This is not always easy to accept, particularly when you have strong reactions to someone. The next time you start losing your cool with your teen, think of it as an opportunity to practice self-control, and remember to thank your teen!

Having power means feeling worthwhile and having a purpose as an individual. We feel good about ourselves when we accomplish something whether we are good at it or not. Notice the reaction on your daughter's face when she passes her driver's license test? How does your son feel when he passes an exam he thought he would fail? Help your teen find purpose by encouraging strengths and interests. Have a look at how you derive power, and see if you are doing all that you can to be purposeful.

We need to feel purposeful in the context of a larger group. How children begin to feel worthwhile to others depends on what they do and the feedback received. If you or others give attention when your teen does something that goes against a rule, such behaviors are indirectly approved. Any attention is better than none, so give attention to socially responsible behaviors.

Freedom of speech and freedom to worship are two examples of humankind's need to live freely among others. The need for freedom is universal, and it is especially important for teenagers who embody the self-centered spirit, at times behaving as if they are the only ones in the world whose needs must be satisfied. By living in the here and now, your teen feels free to seek the greatest good in the shortest time, regardless of the impact on others.

Selfishness has a shelf life. Your teen will learn over time—with incessant help from you and others—that others in the world also have needs. It is about having one foot in the home, attached securely to you, and the other foot outside the home, exploring, playing, seeking inspiration, and connecting with self and others. By following this natural model, your teen will come to understand that with the benefits of freedom come accountability for actions, temperance of desires, and awareness of others' rights.

Your patience will be tested as your teen tests the limits of freedom. It can feel like a never-ending tug-of-war between giving and taking, where taking is usually preferred. It will take time for your teen to find the balance between freedom and responsibility. Remain steadfast, because your efforts will help your teen determine when freedoms can be fully expressed and when self-restraint is recommended. When your teen takes advantage of freedom by overlooking the responsibilities that come with it, see it as a learning opportunity for both of you. The next time it happens, exercise your freedom to step back and take a breath before responding. Refer to this book any time you need support!

Fun is essential to leading a fulfilling life. Through play, children and adults practice life skills and learn about the world around them. Having fun entails pleasure and laughter, both of which are beneficial for learning and healthy for the soul regardless of age. Create opportunities for fun, because many of the moments you will recount later in life will be joyous memories. Rest assured that your teen will not miss such opportunities, because the teenage years are filled with fun activities.

You are probably not aware of all the recreational and leisure activities your teenager engages in, and that is most likely for the best. Jokes played on friends, horseplay with siblings, pranks played on the unwary, and even flirtatious interactions all have their purpose as your teen tries new skills and tests limits and boundaries. Some leisure activities are harmless while others are more risky, but all contain some form of pleasure. They are necessary to obtain feedback from the environment, particularly from peers, romantic interests, and you.

Adolescents do have fun at the expense of others. Banter that is mutually dished out among friends is different from making one peer the brunt of jokes. What a teenager thinks is horseplay could be bullying. Checking in regularly with your teen and inquiring about how free time is spent will allow you to stay on top of your child's activities. This will give you some insight into how your teen fulfills the need for fun and will help you determine whether it is done with others or at the expense of others. Your message is that all parties should be having fun.

Teen Dilemmas

Reasonable decision making is not an adolescent strength. However, as your child transitions from childhood to adulthood, the importance and impact of decisions grow. People are usually given greater responsibility and the freedom to make decisions once they have proven themselves, but in adolescence, the proverbial cart is put before the horse. This seems illogical, but logic has its limits too. Sometimes the best way to learn is to be thrown into a situation and figure it out as you go along. Your teen is perfectly designed to learn by trial and error just as Austin Powers is the right person to save the world from Dr. Evil and Inspector Jacques Clouseau is the detective you want to conduct the most complex investigations. No matter how clumsy or incompetent Powers or Clouseau appear to be, in the end, they get the bad guy or solve the case. Your teen, too, will eventually resolve dilemmas even though at times it may look as if your daughter has no clue or your son is making matters worse.

It is hard to have faith in someone who struggles with the simplest of decisions (such as leaving soiled clothes strewn across the bedroom floor instead of placing them in the laundry basket or not taking dirty plates to the sink when walking by it). Trying to comprehend this can be mind-boggling, so imagine a situation in which the consequence of not doing something is not a redirection or a lecture but being deprived of the opportunity to fulfill an equally important need. Because teens are opportunity seekers who do not discriminate when it comes to fulfilling their needs, this could and often is a common scenario.

A dilemma occurs when one need is met at the expense of another. For your teen, it could be choosing to study for an exam (power) rather than going to a friend's house (fun, belonging, and freedom). If your teen wants to do well academically but equally enjoys spending time with friends, this can be a tough decision. Your teen will greatly appreciate your help in brainstorming options to negotiate a deal whereby all needs can be met. Below is a situation where your teen is asking to go to a friend's house when you know there is an exam the next day. The interaction shows how asking questions can lead your teen to see the situation more objectively without you coming out and saying it.

> Teen: I want to go over to Riley's house.
> *You (Q1): Don't you have a biology test tomorrow?*
> Teen: Yes.
> *You (Q2): When are you going to study?*
> Teen: I already did during study hall.
> *You (Q3): How prepared are you?*
> Teen: I know most of it but need to review some things later.
> *You (Q4): So you still have some studying to do?*
> Teen: Yes.
> *You (Q5): If I were to quiz you now, how well would you do?*
> Teen: I wouldn't know it all. I would still need to study some more, but I can do that when I get back, and you can quiz me later.
> *You: It sounds like you could study more now.*

What did you learn from your questioning? It is clear that your teenager is not completely prepared and at the same time wants to see a friend. You determine that the need for fun, freedom, and belonging seem to be pulling rank on power but not by much. With this information, you can better understand the dilemma instead of becoming angry that your teen would rather hang out with a friend than study. How often have you wanted to spend time with a friend rather than work even though you knew the work needed to be done?

The way you ask questions will determine the type and quality of the responses you receive. In general, limit questions that result in a yes-or-no answer by refraining from asking questions that start with *did you, do you, were you, are you, or have you*. If you want more than a one-word answer, use questions that begin with *how, when, where, why,* or *what*. Even though the questions can be answered with "I don't know," you can still ask for clarification.

Q1 and Q4 are rhetorical questions but useful in that they elicit an affirmative response to help your teen be accountable. The other questions require some explanation, and you gain more information to help your teen understand and resolve the dilemma. What if Q2 had been "Have you studied?" or Q3 had been "Are you prepared?" Both questions would have been answered with a yes, and you wouldn't have detected a dilemma, because you would not have received accurate information. Q3 avoids assumption and encourages self-assessment. Your teen can lie and say that she is all set, but the question requires reflection. Q5 is optional depending on how much you trust your teen's studying habits. Lying will be difficult, because you can easily follow up by quizzing your teen. From the response, more studying is necessary, but one last attempt is made to get your permission to have fun first and study later (fun trumping power).

Let's return to the conversation and see how you can help your teen satisfy both needs.

You: I know you want to hang out with Riley, and you need more time to study. Both are important to you, but which one deserves more attention right now?[1]

Teen: I need to study more.[2]

You: I'm glad you see that. Can you think of any other way to resolve this?[3]

Teen: I can study later when I get back.[4]

You: Is Riley in your class?

Teen: Yes.

You: What about a compromise? You study now until dinner, and then you can go to Riley's for an hour with the expectation of studying.[5]

Teen: Why can't I go now and study later?[6]

You: You want to go to Riley's house, but you also know you need to study more, and you know schoolwork comes first. This allows you to do both, right?[7]

Teen: I guess.

You: The other option is you don't go at all. Which one would you prefer?[8]

Teen: Okay, I'll go study.

You: Great. In an hour, show me what you've done, and you can go to Riley's for an hour after dinner. When you get back, I can quiz you.[9]

---

1 You acknowledge the needs and empower your teen by asking instead of telling her what to do.
2 Your teen knows what choice needs to be made, although it is a difficult one.
3 You acknowledge the responsible choice and have your teen look for other solutions.
4 Your teen is fixated on the original solution. Maybe you agree to your teen's plan, and that is okay.
5 If your teen does not propose this option, you role model creative thinking and compromising.
6 Your proposal is met with resistance, most likely due to the requirements attached.
7 You remind your teen of the dilemma as well as the value of schoolwork to help resolve it.
8 It is helpful to give options and consequences and then give your teen the responsibility of deciding.
9 Will your teen actually study? That is to be determined, but it is better to give the opportunity to be responsible than assume that your teen will not be. Quizzing is not foolproof, but it can act as a safeguard.

In addition to responsible decision making (such as picking up soiled clothes or dirty dishes), the introduction of the dilemma is an even greater challenge. Sometimes there is no easy solution, and the best you can do is listen to your teen's perspective and help determine what needs are driving the behavior. In this example, you reiterated the importance of education, which is a family value. Sometimes values can help prioritize the fulfillment of competing needs. You can offer input and agree on a plan to satisfy both needs or come to accept that a choice must be made, leaving one need momentarily unsatisfied.

Another solution in dealing with complex dilemmas is to allow time to pass. Other factors or realizations that influence a decision may come into play. However, time may be working against your teen if, as in the above example, the exam is the following day. Dilemmas always arise, and the sooner your teen can responsibly cope with them, the easier life will be.

This dilemma resulted in a solution that satisfied all your teen's needs, albeit not the way originally planned. It became satisfactory when compared to the alternative of staying home. The conversation could have deteriorated had you denied the request and imposed your authority. Not acknowledging your teen's needs and examining options would have detracted from the dilemma, built resentment toward you, and denied your teen an opportunity to learn how to weigh interests and compromise when fulfilling competing needs.

In the example, you included a mechanism to prevent your teen from doing nothing for an hour by requiring a review of what had been studied. Even if your teen comes back later and tells you previously known information, it is still practice for the test! It is also a test of trustworthiness, which could have dire consequences for your teen if broken. It is in your teen's interest to comply and do well academically, because the reward is more opportunity to fulfill needs now and down the road when academic achievement translates into a career.

You may think that making an executive decision that emphasizes education enhances the value of learning, but it may have the opposite effect if your teen only sees you exerting authority and disregarding his perspective. If your teen is upset with your decision, not much else may matter; he will focus all attention on you, not on studying. He may purposely do poorly on the test just to spite you. By asking open-ended questions, paraphrasing, and giving options and consequences, you can reasonably discuss opinions. This approach promotes understanding, respect, trust, and support. Within this framework, a healthy relationship will flourish.

A dilemma could arise when your teen is trying to satisfy the same need, such as wanting to join a sports team and the drama club but having to choose one due to a conflict in schedule. Participating in either can satisfy most of the basic needs described, so imagine from your teen's perspective the degree of difficulty in choosing one over the other and the consequences of that choice. Deciding which peer group to belong to, how to derive power, what fun activity to partake in, and how to exercise freedom of expression can cause confusion. You may see this decision as inconsequential, but for the teen who wants it all, this can be a predicament.

Even decisions such as what shirt to wear may not be a question of color coordination or coping with the weather. A seemingly simple decision could affect the needs of belonging, power, freedom, and fun. The more needs that are satisfied by an action, the more important that action becomes. Rejoice when the right shirt is found and is reasonably clean, and be ready to console your teen and seek a creative solution when it's not.

To further complicate your child's decision-making process, your teen may not know which need is being satisfied or which behavior is satisfying which need. The line between what your teen wants and what others want from your child can be blurry. Is the music your teen listens to of interest to her, or is it a favorite because friends listen to it? It could be a combination of both. This also applies to clothing, habits, and hobbies your teen takes up, and it brings to light the importance of how and why needs are fulfilled.

Needs do not diminish with age. Adults are as susceptible to satisfying needs according to familial, social, and cultural norms, possibly disregarding their own desires in the process. How much does the individual influence the group and the group influence the individual? It is a reciprocal relationship in which the individual is always deciding how, collectively or independently, to respond to the group, and the group is perpetually deciding the degree to which it should follow individuals versus adhering to collectively established norms.

Parent Dilemmas

You will be in situations where you want to deny your teen's request. Before outright saying no, think about what needs might be addressed through the activity. The more your teen advocates, begs, and pleads, the greater the chances that the fulfillment of more than one need is in question. If this is the case determine through the use of questions—like in the last example—whether an alternative can be reached so that some of the needs can be met.

Take the classic example of your teen asking to go to a party where there will be no adult supervision. You can assume that there will be exposure to alcohol, explicit content, sexualized behaviors, and possibly drugs. By looking at it from the perspective of your teen's needs, you can see that the party can easily satisfy four out of the five basic needs: belonging, power, freedom, and fun. In your eyes, however, your teen's four needs come at the risk of the one remaining need: survival. Your teen will likely not be in any imminent danger, but the thought of getting into trouble with the law or getting hurt could play with your mind. Giving your child permission to do something you deem questionable comes down to trusting your child's ability to make responsible decisions in light of high-risk situations.

Your teen is already making decisions without your knowledge, so now—while still somewhat under your supervision—is the time for your teen to make mistakes and learn from them. Use this time to be a coach and mentor. Get to know your son. Build trust and confidence in your daughter. You want your teen to come to you when faced with a problem, knowing that you will listen without anger or criticism. Stepping in too many times under the appearance of concern, could come at the expense of breeding insecurity in your child's ability to make decisions. Say no too many times, and you run the risk of your teen lying to you for the sake of being able to do something without fearing your rejection or disapproval.

Here is what a conversation could look like if you say no too often.

> Teen: I want to go over Riley's house.
> *You: Don't you have a history test tomorrow?*
> Teen: No.[10]
> *You: I thought you said there was a test tomorrow.*
> Teen: It was moved to next week to give us more time to study.[11]

---

10 This is a lie. The test is the next day.
11 This is also a lie.

Let's say you told your teenager that she could not go to the unchaperoned party. Your teen tells you instead that she is going to a friend's house, but she goes to the party and gets into trouble. The next day, you say this is exactly why you did not want her to go in the first place. You say, "I knew you were going to make a bad decision, and look what happened!" You were right, your child was wrong, and you now feel proud of your clairvoyant parenting. How effective is this message in furthering your teen's development and your relationship? It is counterproductive: you are in effect saying that your teen is not capable of making responsible decisions in a high-risk situation and that you do not trust her.

Taking an authoritative, black-and-white approach to decision making has the potential to create self-fulfilling prophecies, and it deflates your teen's confidence, diminishing her ability to responsibly fulfill needs. You could now view your child as a liar, further diminishing the needs of belonging and power. You are also inadvertently triggering your teen to take greater risk in fulfilling the needs of freedom and fun in response to your restrictive parenting.

It is important to give your teen opportunities to build self-confidence by making decisions. Be careful what you wish for, and keep the end goal in mind. What type of person are you teaching your teen to be? Your teenager has similar goals as you: to be responsible, trustworthy, and confident. Before engaging with your teen, ask whether the interaction will help build skills and confidence and bring you closer or undermine these critical processes. Highlight and build upon sensible decisions, and give attention when a high-risk situation or dilemma was handled well, even if out of five decisions, only one was handled responsibly.

Expect poor decision making, even in situations that are not all that risky. Mistakes are a necessary part of the learning process for both you and your teen. This does not mean that your child is not trustworthy. Do not consider it an error in judgment or a failure on your teen's part or on your own; openly talk about what can be learned, and make adjustments. Much can be learned from mistakes, and you need to allow them to happen. Be patient and trust the process, and you will both benefit.

Exchanging the Baton

Your teen will not always perform as you wish. This is okay. There could be an exam tomorrow, but maybe your teen isn't feeling up to studying (power). Your son could be thinking about an upcoming date (fun, power, freedom, and belonging). If you have other things on your mind, concentration and performance on another task may not be optimal. The desire to fulfill a need fluctuates and depends on how recently or how often energy is put into fulfilling it. If your daughter studied for two hours for a chemistry test and also has to study for a history test, she may need to do something else before studying for history. Having a bite to eat (survival), calling a friend (fun and belonging), or doing nothing for a few minutes (freedom) may take precedence. Prioritizing and becoming efficient at satisfying needs comes with experience.

The process of becoming more independent can be compared to the transition point in relay running when the first runner (you) approaches the end of the final lap at high speed, baton (responsibility) in hand, focused on maintaining speed and performance (hopes and wishes), and trusting that the second runner (your teen) will meet expectations. All you can do when you hand over responsibility is trust that your teenager will manage. Even with all your experience, you can still encounter difficulties when dealing with a conflict of needs, so imagine the struggles that may arise during adolescence.

Accidents and unforeseen events can change a situation before you have time to make adjustments. Expect the baton to be dropped—it does not mean you should call it quits or consider your efforts failures. It means that more practice is required. Continue handing over the baton.

Over time, your anxieties will lower, and your teen will confidently hold the baton and run to her potential, knowing that you are championing her efforts. Life consists of trial and error. It is a placating but false belief that adults have it all figured out and that teens are helplessly lost and clueless. We can feel lost or question long-held beliefs at any point in life. Because teens are more flexible, your teen may be better at handling uncertainty than you. Do not project your worries onto your child, and learn to differentiate between your concerns and those of your teen. Has worrying about something over which you have no control ever improved a situation?

Your life may be demanding, and although you wish your child to always behave in a manner you deem appropriate, this will not always happen. Such unrealistic expectations are a setup and will only lead to unhappiness. Embrace your teen's woes. They may trigger similar issues within you, because we all share the same needs and the dilemmas that accompany them. Just as your teen may remind you of an unresolved issue, he may hold the key to helping you get closer to solving it. At times you are better off watching your teen practice and letting him take the lead and hand you the baton.

What You Can Learn from Understanding Your Teenager's Needs

Teenagers are the ultimate need-fulfilling machines, yearning to connect with their innate abilities and with others. There is no better life stage than adolescence to seek inspiration in this department. Teens are insatiable in their desire to explore interests and push physical, mental, emotional, institutional, and societal limits. You can watch with awe how your teenager navigates life, moving fluidly from the fulfillment of one need to the next without restraint or regard for consequences. Your daughter's urge to do whatever is needed at the moment will have you wondering where she got the idea that the world revolves around her, but at the same time, it can leave you amazed. Hold your judgment for a moment, and learn from the pro.

What needs have you left unfulfilled? Maybe you are short of sleep and exercise (survival). No one assures that the need for sleep is satisfied like your teenager. If you find yourself tired then rest. It could mean changing your routine and schedule, but an extra hour of sleep may help you be more productive and efficient. Longer waking hours do not automatically equate to greater productivity.

Image and appearance are important to teens, and much of their time goes into looking good. Your fitness is important. Just as your teen may engage in regular sports or physical activities, you benefit physically and mentally from regular exercise. If you make it a priority, you will find the time. If your teen wants to do something, you can guarantee that it will be done one way or another.

Your teenager looks to satisfy the need for belonging outside of your home. Follow in your teen's footsteps. Call friends and find groups, activities, and clubs to partake in now that you spend less time satisfying this need for your child and have more time for yourself. Be courageous. Experiment with new ways of fitting in, the way that your teen does, by finding ways of belonging that you always had an interest in but never had the time or nerve to pursue. Now is the time for you to take action.

The one need that comes full circle for parents of teens is the need for power. Just as your teen is beginning to define who he is and how he wants others to see him, you could be asking yourself the same question as you approach or settle into midlife. You derive a high degree of self-worth in your role as a parent, but that diminishes as your child develops and depends less on you. The more balanced you are in fulfilling all of your needs (and not relying solely on your parenting role), the easier it will be to cope with the eventual empty-nest stage. How else do you gain self worth and feel worthwhile others?

Just as your teen is constantly reassessing needs with age, so should you. How twelve-year-olds fulfill needs changes when they are seventeen. You are a parent for a lifetime, but with time your role diminishes as well as how you go about fulfilling your needs. Socrates said, "The unexamined life is not worth living." I prefer to say that the examined life is worth living! Take the time to examine your needs outside your roles of parenting and your profession. Life is not just about parenting and working. Take a tip from your teenager, and discover all that you are by exploring, playing, being inspired, and connecting with yourself and others.

As your teen spreads her wings, savoring the freedoms that come with adolescence, she requires less supervision. You will have more free time to do what you want (or once did) to help you be more of who you are. Your teenager has little restraint when it comes to exercising her rights and freedoms, and now you can conduct yourself in a similar manner. As you learn to let go of your teen, you can regain the freedom you felt as an adolescent. The empty-nest syndrome does not have to mean that you are alone, left to sob and worry about your child. Spread your own wings; the world is for you to take as well.

If you feel that fun has been missing in your life, who better to ask than someone who knows you well and is an expert in having fun! Ask your teen for some tips if you are feeling in need of an escape. Teens are insatiable pleasure seekers, so observing your teen may give you ideas on how to let loose and have fun. Most likely your teen fulfills the need for fun in the company of others, so pick up the phone and arrange an activity with a friend. All work and no play makes life exhausting and boring. Fun does not have to be scheduled into your daily routine. It can be spontaneous and an integral part of your day by making it a priority, in the same way that you make sleep and exercise a priority for a healthy, balanced life.

As a parent, you often sacrifice your needs to satisfy your child's. You can only do this to a certain extent without negative consequences. Your needs are important. The selfless choices you make for the benefit of your child can become unhealthy if you find yourself ignoring your basic needs. Just as your teen must learn to properly fulfill his needs, do not neglect your obligation to satisfy your own.

Take the time to care for yourself. If you find yourself lacking hours in the day, turn to your teen for advice on how to better plan, coordinate, and execute. You may be surprised at the response or even discover that your teen is feeling the same way. Before you know it, you may find ways to fulfill the same need together. Satisfying multiple needs together is even better. If cooking is the activity chosen, a case could be made that all five needs are being satisfied (survival being the fifth). These memorable experiences can be repeated when your teen is an adult.

Understanding the needs of your child and yourself can improve your lives as individuals and bring you closer as a family. Take a closer look at how each of you satisfies your needs. Where are there points of overlap? Use them as areas to learn. The goal is to strike a healthy balance—not necessarily fifty-fifty but an equilibrium where you feel you are getting enough of your needs met as an individual. This will give you the energy, confidence, and attitude to continue helping your child to learn to responsibly identify and satisfy needs.

Lesson 1 Highlights

Five Basic Needs
- We all behave to satisfy these basic needs:
  - Survival—food, clothing, shelter, and overall health
  - Belonging—connecting physically and emotionally with others
  - Power—feeling worthwhile to self and others
  - Freedom—having a sense of autonomy
  - Fun—enjoying life, learning, relaxing, and energizing
- The more needs that are satisfied by an action, the more important that action is in contributing to your well-being.

Teen Dilemmas
- Conflict resulting from the inability to fulfill the same or multiple needs due to time constraints or other barriers can present as stress or anger.
- Help your teen by organizing dilemmas into a "needs and consequences" perspective, and allow time to choose.

Parent Dilemmas
- When deciding whether or not to allow your teen to do something, consider your teen's needs and at minimum negotiate a reasonable solution.
- Being too restrictive (or taking an authoritative approach) can increase the chances of your teen becoming untruthful and taking greater risks.

Exchanging the Baton
- Continue giving your teen opportunities to make important choices to improve decision making, trust, and confidence.
- Accept that poor decisions will happen, and do not let worries turn into self-fulfilling prophecies.

What You Can Learn from Understanding Your Teenager's Needs
- Fulfill your own needs by learning from your teen, who is always on the hunt for opportunities to satisfy needs.
- If you are having difficulty fulfilling a need, ask your teen how to do so. Maybe your teen joins you because the idea is interesting.

Lesson 2:
Examining Values

Your beliefs become your thoughts,
Your thoughts become your words,
Your words become your actions,
Your actions become your habits,
Your habits become your values,
Your values become your destiny.

        Mahatma Gandhi

The Value of Values

Values are personal and social ideals that we adopt, alter, and abandon over time with the goal of defining who we are and how we want others to see us.[12] If our needs motivate us to behave, our values guide us in how we go about fulfilling those needs. For example, both you and your teen are hungry (survival), but your teen is a vegetarian, and you are not. Your values will result in your teen eating a veggie burger while you devour a bacon cheeseburger. Pay attention to how values influence how your teen satisfies his needs. Your reaction to your teen, whether favorable, indifferent, or disapproving, is not based on what your child is trying to accomplish (needs) but rather how he is going about doing it (values).

---

12 Refer to the list of values at the end of the lesson.

Say that you walk into the kitchen to find the refrigerator door wide open and your teen chugging directly from the milk container—but wait, there's more! You notice an open container of food, a used plate and fork, and crumbs littering the counter. All are signs of a hasty attempt to fill the belly. Just as you are about to say something, your teen quickly shoves the uncapped milk container onto the shelf, slams the refrigerator door, and whizzes by you with a guilty but cordial smile. Standing in a daze, you wonder why your teen couldn't take a minute to tidy up when you have mentioned it a hundred times.

What you respond to emotionally, behaviorally, physiologically, and intellectually is not the fact that your child was hungry and needed to eat something. It is the way that your teen went about fulfilling this need and how the behavior flew in the face of the values you have been preaching since childhood: respect, cleanliness, manners, and helpfulness. Why doesn't your teen get it after years of indoctrination?

The powers at work are as great as your determination to create a responsible and mature young adult. Do not despair. Your efforts are not in vain; you are dealing with a case of competing needs and values. A quick analysis would say that your child values disorder, poor etiquette, and selfishness, to name a few stereotypical teenage traits. Remember that as your teen fled—with a full stomach—a more pressing need required attention. If survival needs are met regularly without concern, your teen may take eating for granted, reducing the act to a means to fulfill a more pressing need such as fun, freedom, power, and belonging. The values that influence how your teen fulfills needs are the source of your frustration, not your teen.

When needs compete, time and values become deciding factors, and the more pressing need will take precedence. In this case, the mess in the kitchen made it apparent how needs, time, and values influenced your teen's choices. Chowing down was the priority. Leaving a mess was a consequence, but it allowed more time to meet up with friends, which easily ranked higher than cleaning. The values of friendship, autonomy, and adventure overshadowed the values of consideration, manners, and cleanliness.

If your teen had to study for a biology test in lieu of meeting up with friends, it is possible that your child would have picked up afterwards because there may have been no rush to fulfill the need to study. In that case, the need of survival (eating) and belonging (cleaning up) would have trumped power (studying for the biology test). The values of consideration and cleanliness associated with the former need would have trumped academic achievement (values associated with the latter). The message is that by understanding your child's needs and values, you can remind yourself that, in most cases, your teenager's behaviors are not attempts to make you feel a certain way.

What You Value Counts

You may regard the mess in the kitchen as disrespectful and lecture your teen on how it affects you and others who use the kitchen. It is okay to voice your feelings as long as you value connection and understanding. Doing so allows you to assert your values and helps you understand and acknowledge your teen's values. If the conversation has a confrontational focus, you turn it into a "you versus me" situation where the mess was a direct attack on you. Taking this one-sided approach harms your relationship and condones the behaviors you wish to stop. Is there a difference between a tirade about how the messy kitchen affects you and your teen who left the mess to attend to a more pressing need? Both promote a self-centered focus.

Like you, your teen wants to be understood and may feel that you have difficulty doing this. How many times have you heard, "Mom, you don't understand"? How many times have you said to your teen, "You just don't get it"? Demonstrate your ability to understand your teen, address a behavior and attitude you disapprove of, and you can come out smelling like roses, because the focus is on your teen's behavior and the impact it has on everybody, not just you. Acknowledge your teen's needs and values to show that you can relate to her situation. From there, you can voice your dismay about the way the needs were fulfilled. You can revisit the values you wish to promote, all the while supporting your teen in developing her values.

A few hours have passed since your child blew by you after leaving chaos in the kitchen. Your teen enters the kitchen to grab a bite to eat after having spent a fun-filled afternoon swimming with friends. You are preparing a delicious dinner and want to address what happened earlier. The mess is still on the counter. Below are two hypothetical responses with different outcomes. The first example shows a parent—not you—personalizing the incident.

> Teen: Hi, we had a really good time!
> *Parent yelling: I had a great time too coming home to your mess!*[13] *You can be so thoughtless and selfish! Do you think I am your maid?*[14]
> Teen: No.
> *Parent continuing to yell: Why did you leave the kitchen a mess?*
> Teen: I don't know. My friends were waiting for me.[15]

---

13 Parent is sarcastic, disregards the child's excitement and enthusiasm, and focuses on self.
14 Parent personalizes the behavior, becoming self-absorbed, and tries to make the teen feel guilty.
15 As the parent attacks, the teen has three options: shut down, counterattack, or defend. The teen chooses to defend, which could be an interpersonal dynamic between the two when such incidents occur.

Examining Values | 27

> *Parent: Who did you think was going to pick it up?*[16]
> Teen: I was going to pick it up when I got back.
> *Parent: Really? I doubt that! I work all day and have to come home to your mess.*[17] *Pick up after yourself so I don't have to yell and scream so much! Now set the table!*[18]
> Teen, *putting head down, speaking in a submissive tone*: Okay.

As long as the parent continues to let his or her emotions be controlled by the teen's answers, the parent will become angrier with each response. It is a trap that will capture both of them. What values did the parent promote during this interaction? How do these values affect the teenager's need for power, freedom, fun, and belonging? How do interactions like this affect the relationship over time?

The values expressed in the interaction were selfishness, loss of control, degradation, doubt, and lack of trust. Now emotionally frustrated, physically drained, and psychologically deflated, the teen shuffles to the counter, cleans up, leaves, and returns moments later to eat. How do you think dinner went?

In this scenario, you demonstrate values that appropriately address the issue while showing support, not personalizing the incident, and maintaining the relationship.

> Teen: Hi. We had a really good time!
> *You: I'm sure. It's so nice outside. What did you do?*[19]

---

16 Parent implies that the teen is purposely doing this to give the parent more work.
17 Parent immediately diminishes the teen's confidence and self-worth.
18 Parent irresponsibly blames the teen for his or her reaction and then gives a command.
19 You show interest in your teen's day and seek to find out more. What values are you promoting?

Teen: The water was great, and we met other friends there. We all had fun diving off the dock, playing volleyball, and hanging out.[20]

You: Well, it sounds like you had a good time.[21]

Teen: It was a blast. We're planning to go again next weekend. I'm looking forward to it. I think the same group will be there and maybe a few others as well.

You, looking at the mess on the counter: You know, you forgot to do something when you rushed out of here, smiling at me.[22]

Teen: Yes, I know.[23]

You: I support you having fun with your friends, but the expectation is that you pick up after yourself and respect spaces that we all share. I was disappointed to see the kitchen a mess when I returned from work.[24]

Teen: I know. I was in a rush, and they were waiting for me.[25]

You: It is your responsibility to take care of what needs to be done at home before going out with friends. As I said, I'm all for you having a good time with friends, but I expect you to follow through with what's expected here, so what can I expect next time?[26]

Teen: I'll pick up and not leave a mess before leaving.

---

20 Your openness and interest encourage further sharing.
21 You listen by reiterating your teen's sentiments and responding to responsible actions, not just negative ones.
22 You combine a subtle nonverbal gesture and bring up the issue in a way that acknowledges your teen's awareness of it in a nonconfrontational manner.
23 As a result, your teen takes responsibility.
24 You reiterate your teen's needs and values as well as your disappointment that basic rules were not followed.
25 Although guilty as charged, your teen attempts to find an excuse.
26 You remain calm, ignoring the excuse and bring the conversation back to values and expectations. You have your teen verbalize the expectation to help internalize it.

> *You: Great. Now please clean up before it turns into a science project.[27] Afterward I could use some help with dinner.*
> Teen: Okay.
> *You: Can you please chop vegetables or set the table?[28]*
> Teen: I'll set the table. What's for dinner?

How do the scenarios differ in addressing the issue and caring for the relationship? The first addresses only the parent's needs and values (promoting the stereotypical self-centered adolescent mind-set), while in the second, you acknowledge your teen's experience and perspective. The first is an emotional tirade, while the second is a conversation that involves healthy components of communication—Lesson 6—such as listening, acknowledging, rephrasing, being nonjudgmental, and allowing time to reflect.

In the second dialogue, you remind your teen of limits, values, and expectations. You do not let feelings guide your behaviors. What would your family look like if everyone reacted on emotion or justified behaviors because of what they think others were doing to them?

Your initial reaction may have been similar to that of the first parent, but before addressing the issue, you gathered yourself and had clear goals in mind. You modeled healthy values such as responsibility, connection, empathy, self-control, respect, cooperation, helpfulness, harmony, acknowledgment, understanding, and humor. These values influenced your conduct and greatly influenced the outcome.

Your priority was your child and household expectations, not how the mess affected your life. You made this clear by acknowledging your teen as he entered the room, showing that even though

---
27 Humor helps depersonalize the situation, showing that you are disappointed with the behavior, not with your teen.
28 You politely give a choice as to how to be helpful, emphasizing values that were earlier disregarded.

you are upset, you value and respect him as a person. After your acknowledgment, you listened to your teen's account of the time spent with friends, which led to him to tell you more about the afternoon. This encouraged dialogue, and again the priority for you was the relationship—showing your teenager that you are present and listening and, most importantly, that you care, regardless of the mess in the kitchen.

Once these fundamental values associated with humanness were established, you addressed the issue. You acknowledged your teen's needs and values, showed respect, and shifted the focus to the needs of others who live in the home. This reiterates that just as your teen wants to be valued and respected, so do others. This reproach has nothing to do with being a "maid" and working long hours but with upholding the expectation of being considerate by picking up after oneself.

You were also nonjudgmental. Passing judgment, which occurred in the first example, damages self-esteem. You stuck to the facts and did not attack your teenager's character. You reminded your teen of established values and expectations and, for a third time, showed support of his needs and values. You used a follow-up question, asking how your teen will act next time. Questions that require an interpretation are optional, depending on your child's maturity level or the seriousness of the matter. They can be helpful to see whether he is paying attention. Your question was not, "Do you understand?" Such a question would have generated a yes for the sake of quickly ending the conversation without your teen internalizing the expectation and values.

Next comes humor, a value your teen most likely appreciates. Humor can help lighten the mood and show your teen that you are not personalizing his behaviors. It is a means for you to get your point across indirectly. When used appropriately, humor can be an effective tool. However, using it excessively can make it difficult for your child to take you seriously, or it can turn into bitter sarcasm, sending a contradictory message, like in the first response. The next time a mess is left, you may only have to reference the science project as a reminder to pick it up. If you are lucky, your teen may even clean up with a smile.

Finally, you politely asked your teen to pick up and help with dinner. Your teen appreciated the way you handled the interaction and continued the conversation by asking about dinner, sending the message that he is not upset at you for being a parent. Playing with values and testing limits is your teen's job. It is your job to manage these behaviors in a helpful manner.

You may be wondering, "Who can respond this way all the time?" Parenting can be tiring. It is natural that you will show symptoms of the first parent. Emotions can get the best of anybody, so when you snap, do damage control by teaching the values of processing and making repairs. You can talk about the incident later when you are both calm. Explain why you reacted the way you did and apologize for your inappropriate reaction. You can turn any interaction into a teaching moment. Losing your patience becomes problematic only if you cannot apologize or if you are often reactive. Apologies and explanations lose their meaning if you repeatedly lose your temper. How often can you hear your child apologize for a behavior over and over?

Examining Values over Time

You are continuously constructing a belief system that exemplifies who you are by adding or removing values learned from education, experiences, and observations. Your personality and tendencies also influence your values. If by nature you are always on the go, you may value swiftness, action, and productivity. Your belief system will influence the way you view your child's actions, what values you teach your child, and how you interact with your child. Your values become a part of the lens through which you interpret the world.

Without warning, you may be forced to reevaluate your belief system due to a sudden life-changing event such as losing a job or grieving the abrupt death of a loved one. Having a medical condition still means that you must eat, but it may force you to change your values regarding nutrition and physical fitness. Even welcome unexpected events such as a marriage proposal, an out-of-state job offer, or the birth of a child may make you reevaluate the importance you place on certain values.

Like needs, values may compete with each other. One day your teen may bring home a love interest that you do not approve of. Your disapproval may stem from reasons that challenge your values about dating and partnership. This relationship may run counter to several different values; such as competing with your values of acceptance, putting family first, and supporting your teen's happiness. Another example concerns academics. Say that your teen has been accepted to a school that specializes in a field of study she adamantly wants to pursue, but the school offers little financial aid. She has also been accepted to a college with a fantastic financial aid package, but the school does not offer the same area of specialization. Your decision will be influenced by your values, whether they are frugality and financial stability or empathy, self-determination, empowerment, and autonomy.

Your teen's response to the decision, if she has a say (yet another value), will also depend on her values. If financial independence is important, she may forgo the expensive school and find more cost-effective ways to gain the desired education. If career pulls rank, the decision may be to take out a large loan and trust that the right career development will pay off over time.

It is okay to impart your core values, but realize that your teenager is an individual who needs your support in finding his way in accordance with who he is. Stepping back and giving your teenager the space to develop his own set of values will permit you to have a look at your own. Just as your teen may feel pressure from you or society concerning what values to uphold, you too may feel obligated to uphold values for the same reason. Now is your chance to reassess your values to determine whether they are in line with who you are or if they have been adopted solely out of familial, social, or cultural traditions.

This process can lead to shedding layers of unhealthy patterns from your own youth. This translates into action leading you to live more in accordance with your nature. These changes may be socially acceptable, such as quitting smoking and joining a fitness club in order to become more physically fit. What others might think of you (or how they may treat you) because of a starkly different belief from that of family, friends, coworkers, or a loved one could be more difficult to manage. Imagine the criticism that could result from an unconventional change such as quitting a stable, well-paying job with great benefits, selling your home, emptying your savings, and dipping into your retirement account to buy an old, decrepit home in order to live your lifelong dream of owning a bed and breakfast.

The cost of not listening to your inner voice may be greater than a scornful remark from an onlooker. The more closely your beliefs align with who you are, the more inner peace you will have, regardless of the commotion that may be going on around you. Keep this in mind when supporting your teenager, whose values may run counter to family and social norms. When it comes to examining your values and the challenges that arise from the process, you have more in common with your teen than you think.

Overcoming Limitations of Values

Values can become rigid if you are not open to seeing the world through different lenses. Fortunately, with every generation comes a new collective attitude, most likely in response to a world view that no longer resonates with the realities that younger people face. Adults who can adopt the attitudes of newer generations can be open-minded and adapt to changing global perceptions. Taking on new values at midlife could disrupt well-established routines and rattle your comfort zone, but doing so will make you part of a new and exciting ideology rather than holding on to an old and expired one.

As helpful as it is to let your values influence how you fulfill your needs, rigidity in your value system can prevent you from developing. It can cause tension in your relationship, particularly if some of your teen's values differ from yours, which is often the case. To overcome this limitation, appreciate your child's belief system, realizing that it will change and, in the end, will most likely not mirror yours. Your value system will evolve as well, particularly if you are yearning to be more of who you truly are.

If you feel the need to become friendlier, add friendliness to your list of values, and brainstorm ways to turn your values into behaviors. Maybe you would like to have new experiences but are generally not daring; add adventure to your list, and support that value by trying activities that require courage. If the new value resonates within you, it will become an integral part of who you are.

Core values are essential as guiding principles, but explore other values that are underdeveloped. Think of them as seeds planted in the past, possibly a part of your genetic predisposition, that require water, fertilizer, and sunlight to grow. It is healthy to want to learn regardless of your age, and doing so will help you keep a youthful mind, body, and soul. You can expand your thoughts, engage in new behaviors, and experience different feelings by adding a new value or nurturing a preexisting value. Don't let outdated values get in the way of your development. Adopt values that support both you and your teen's growth.

What You Can Learn from Your Teenager's Values

Like you, your teen is trying to figure out how to best go about satisfying needs that are in alignment with her values and beliefs. Your teen is simultaneously testing different belief systems coming from various sources. It may be difficult at times to understand your teen's choices; experimenting with different values from one day to the next, your daughter may appear fickle. Seeing your teen's choices as sampling will keep you from criticizing or dismissing a belief that runs counter to your established ways.

Deviating from the norm can mean stepping out of your comfort zone, and that can be awkward. If you find there are differences between your value system and that of your child, there is no need to panic. This should be the case. Discuss these differences as opposed to criticizing them. Look more closely at your teen's values. You might learn something about your teen and yourself.

Try not to take your teen's behaviors at face value. If you are irked by something your teen has done, identify what need is trying to be met, and figure out the values that are guiding the behaviors. Once you have done that, apply your child's needs and values to yourself, and see what you come up with. Your teen comes home from a day at the amusement park and tells you about his wild experience on the roller coaster. The need here is clearly fun, but it could also be a need for power if your teen feels a sense of worth or pride in overcoming an intimidating ride. If his peers are going on the ride, the need to belong could also be at work. It could even satisfy the need for freedom, because the moments of feeling weightless could replicate the soaring sensation of flying.

Taking all that into consideration, look at some of the values that could be associated with deciding to go on the roller coaster to satisfy these needs: friendship, adventure, courage, challenge, curiosity, recognition, and risk taking. Instead of passing judgment and dismissing the roller coaster as reckless, think of an activity for yourself that satisfies the needs for fun, freedom, power, and belonging. Apply the values you came up with from your teen, and convert all of that into an activity. How does that sit with you? Let's assume that you are not a roller coaster aficionado, but maybe you enjoy rock climbing or paragliding. If you do like roller coasters, schedule a time to ride one with your teen. Doing so will validate his values, and to top it all off, you will both have a great memory to share.

There will be times when your teen's values shock you. You may one day observe your child satisfying a need driven by a value you instilled and the next day watch the same need being satisfied in a manner that boggles your mind, making you wonder if this is the child you raised. You may question your effectiveness as a parent, wondering what you were teaching all those years. If you have a strong reaction to a value your teen is expressing, one that does not reflect who you think you are, look within yourself, and ask what personal chord is being struck within you. What can be learned?

Your teen's behavior could be something you outwardly do not condone but inwardly have a desire to do. If this is not the case, challenge yourself and analyze a value your teen espouses. Pick one that you do not embrace. It does not necessarily have to be one that triggers a worrisome reaction; it just needs to pique your interest.

Write that value on a piece of paper, and carry it with you. For the next week, turn this value into an action once a day. Take note of the thoughts and feelings you had while engaged in the activity. What need is the value influencing most? Is it a need that you have been neglecting? You may unlock a door to a buried desire or discover something new about yourself. You will challenge yourself and further your understanding of your teen. If for no other reason, try it for the sake of strengthening your relationship.

My boys like mountain biking, and as adolescents, they are more courageous when faced with challenging terrain. I look for the easy path, and if I see them having difficulty, I assume that it is best to dismount and walk through the obstacle. Occasionally I adopt the values of courage and risk taking. When I do there is a physiological change when climbing over fallen limbs or pedaling uphill over rocky trails with my palms sweating, heart pounding, and muscles straining. I become more attentive when riding. Sometimes I make it, and sometimes I don't.

I have realized that the outcome is not important. Trying to take on an obstacle while attached to a bike is exciting and fun regardless of whether I succeed or fail. Falling down is not pleasant, but it can be funny afterward when my boys recount how I went down in a heap. We chat about our triumphs and failures, boasting about the former and laughing about the latter. By taking on the values of courage and risk taking, I more satisfactorily fulfilled the needs of fun, freedom, belonging, and power, and our relationship strengthens through an activity we all enjoy.

As long as your child's way of interacting with the world is neither irresponsible nor harmful, support your teen's development. For example, if you are more of a rational person, you will probably encourage your child to thoroughly examine the pros and cons of decisions and behaviors. However, it could be that your teen is not the cerebral type and is more adept at trusting her instincts. Maybe she makes decisions based on a gut feeling, sometimes having a hard time explaining why she did something and stating that it felt like the right thing to do. Such decision making can be confused with rashness, but be careful not to judge too quickly. It could be that your child's intuitive tendency, in its early stages of development, manifests as impulsivity. With time, experience, and your encouragement, your teen will learn how to value and proficiently use this ability.

Although you will instill a portion of your values in your child, it is necessary to support other values your teen embraces as a result of his education, experiences, or personality, even though they may not be ones you practice. As your teen begins to differentiate from you and others, look beyond the outcome of his behaviors and pay attention to the process, because this is what makes your teen unique. Values connect and differentiate us. Spend less time judging your teen's values and more time fostering those values that resonate with him, even if they run counter to what you follow. Use your teenager as a role model. You have a great opportunity to discover (or become reacquainted) with values that may lead you to becoming more effective as a parent and are more in line with who you are.

Examining Values

List of Values

Achievement	Adventure	Autonomy
Balance	Beauty	Belonging
Bravery	Challenge	Change
Clarity	Community	Commitment
Compassion	Competition	Composure
Confidence	Connection	Cooperation
Craftiness	Creativity	Credibility
Curiosity	Dependability	Desire
Determination	Diversity	Empathy
Enthusiasm	Ethical conduct	Excellence
Fairness	Fame	Family
Fitness	Flexibility	Forgiveness
Freedom	Friendship	Fun
Genuineness	Happiness	Helping others
Honesty	Humility	Humor
Inner harmony	Integrity	Intuition
Knowledge	Leadership	Love
Loyalty	Making a difference	Mastery
Meaningful work	Nature	Open-mindedness
Order	Partnership	Patience
Perseverance	Privacy	Recognition
Reputation	Responsibility	Risk taking
Security	Self-control	Self-expression
Self-respect	Selflessness	Service
Spirituality	Strength	Trust
Wealth	Well-being	Wisdom

Lesson 2 Highlights

The Value of Values
- Values guide us in how we go about fulfilling our needs.
- Support rather than personalize or criticize the values your teen is experimenting with that can run counter to your own and result in inconsistent behaviors.

What You Value Counts
- You are always demonstrating your value system. Express and experiment with values that support the relationship and your development.
- Use humor in moderation to deal with tough issues, and show that you value responsibility when you respond inappropriately by apologizing and explaining.

Examining Values over Time
- Changing your values requires objectivity, self-examination, and the courage to go against tradition or cultural norms.
- Even if you do not want to examine your values, unforeseen life events can force you to do so, and this can drastically change how you relate to yourself and others.

Overcoming Limitations of Values
- Avoid being too set in your ways (which results in personal and relationship stagnation) by acknowledging and respecting differing values in others.

- When you embrace new values, practice them regularly through action in order for the belief to become an integral part of who you are.

What You Can Learn from Your Teenager's Values
- The courage to adopt a new belief brings growth opportunities for your relationship and you.
- For one week, take ownership of a value that your teen holds that intrigues you, and act upon it daily, recording how it impacts the fulfillment of your needs.

Lesson 3:
EPIC Existence

Live with intention. Walk to the edge. Listen hard. Practice wellness. Play with abandon. Laugh. Choose with no regret. Do what you love. Live as if this is all there is.
         Mary Anne Radmacher-Hershey

How Philosophy Simplifies Parenting

About two thousand years ago, the Stoic philosopher Epictetus (AD 55–135) was born into slavery and later banished from Rome, and the circumstances of his life rivaled the lives of the disadvantaged youth with whom I worked. Instead of succumbing to the life he was born into, he learned from it and espoused a philosophy that is useful in developing the relationship you want with your teen. Epictetus came to believe that anyone could obtain contentment, regardless of what happens, because we are always in control of our attitudes and responses. Epictetus took this belief a step further. He said that we should embrace the difficult problems life haphazardly throws at us, because they are mental exercises and opportunities for spiritual growth.

 This is fabulous news, because there are no shortages of challenges when accompanying your child through preadolescence to young adulthood. The next time you have a challenging moment with your teen, instead of having a strong emotional reaction, thank her for the wonderful opportunity to gain wisdom and grow spiritually! You may be acquainted with the well-known interpretation of Epictetus's philosophy, also known as the Serenity Prayer:

> God, grant me the serenity to accept
> the things I cannot change,
> Courage to change the things I can,
> And wisdom to know the difference.

To gain knowledge in differentiating between what is in your control and what is not, Epictetus advised accepting the true nature of things. He professed that suffering arises when you regulate that which is uncontrollable and fail to exert your influence over that which you have authority. Applying this philosophy to your teenager, the questions become the following: What is your teen's true nature? What real control do you have over him? How can you come to accept who she is? Once you answer these questions, you can move closer to understanding what is in your control and what is not. Discerning between the two allows you to focus your energy on the former.

Think of the last confrontation you had with your teen. How much of your emotional, mental, and physical energy was focused on things over which you had no control? If you displayed heightened emotions, loud or incoherent speech, and erratic behavior, you most likely focused on what you could not control—your teen. If you were stable emotionally, mentally, and physically, you likely focused on what you could control—you.

If it is your teen's nature to act impulsively, you have no control over when your teen makes an imprudent decision, one that may result in an undesirable consequence for your child and for you. It is helpful to accept this aspect of your teen and provide outlets to learn from these tendencies. If your teen inadvertently locks the keys in the car, what is the benefit of responding in anger to a situation that you know can occur at any time, even to yourself? Was your teen's plan to inconvenience and upset you? It likely bothered your teen as much it did you.

This is not to say that you should dismiss such events altogether, particularly if they occur often, but expect events like this to happen every now and then. When they do, you can respond in a manner that fosters understanding and learning. Would you rather have your teen accidentally lock the keys in the car or purposely lock you out of her life because you cannot control your emotions when she does something in her nature but not to your liking?

Something else you should not dismiss is a natural model of learning your teen uses on a daily basis. I witnessed its use hundreds of times with the youth I worked with and with my sons. Adults often misinterpret the EPIC model of development, which consists of four components: Explore, Play, Inspire, and Connect. To completely embrace your teenager, let's look at a process that can help you improve your parenting and live a more fulfilling life.

Explore

The human mind, body, and spirit were designed for the sake of discovering. *Explore* is the first of four traits that come standard in teens, and is useful in adulthood when one is taking on life's challenges and obstacles. The moment a toddler becomes mobile, the explorative nature takes a gigantic leap forward. Instead of relying on the parent to bring the world to him, the toddler can now bring the world to himself. Even barriers such as gates, cribs, fences, or the grabbing hands of a concerned adult cannot deter the unwavering desire to embark on endless search-and-discover missions. Barriers become easier to overcome as the cunning adolescent mind develops and curiosity and ingenuity grow with experience.

Most, if not all, of our basic needs are fulfilled through exploration. Beginning with our early ancestors, the basic acts of survival, hunting, and gathering relied on exploration, whether it was tracking evasive prey or finding new sources and varieties of fruits, berries, or other vegetation. Even today the act of finding a job (commonly referred to as job hunting), is a form of exploration. An interview is an explorative attempt to learn what the job entails, how your skills will be used, what the work environment will be like, and how you will fit in with colleagues. Trying new foods is a form of exploration, as is looking for a suitable place to live (house hunting).

In regard to belonging, particularly in childhood and adolescence, we search for others who share similar beliefs or interests. Exploration is the most basic form of learning, and we typically like doing it in the company of others. When we are with friends, loved ones, or coworkers, we try out new things and share new ideas and experiences. This can include trying a new restaurant, playing a new game, visiting a unknown place, or working on a new project. In romantic relationships, we explore creative ways to be intimate and keep the relationship exciting. If you think of memorable moments in your life when you did something for the first time, it was probably done with someone else.

Fulfilling our need for power by meeting a goal or overcoming a challenge is also an explorative process. A new tool or skill set was probably what helped you grow and learn. Any discovery uncovered as a result of exploration leads to self-worth. In feeling worthwhile to others, whether in your family or as part of a team, a discovery, a solution, or a novel idea will result in recognition and appreciation by the group that also benefits from the find.

Exploration is a manifestation of freedom, and freedom allows for exploration. There is a great sense of liberty when one is exploring, knowing that there are always new possibilities and novel things to unearth—an unknown plant, animal, or planet, an invention to help simplify daily life, or a cure for a disease. Exploration allows us to feel free rather than bound by laws, rules, or norms. Freedom allows us to find innovative ways to use known objects or build upon and even challenge widely held beliefs. Exploring allows us the freedom to discover for the sake of posterity, and in the process gives us the liberty to become comfortable in our own skin.

Having fun can mean engaging in an activity with a good friend. For young people, it can entail doing something unknown or putting a new twist on something familiar to kick up the thrill factor. A good example is "geocaching," a global and technological take on the age-old explorative scavenger hunt, which traditionally occurred in your backyard and only with children. The modernized version has people of all ages and countries seeking containers, called geocaches, using global positioning devices to provide coordinates and clues. The anticipation while exploring is exciting, because you do not know how long it will take you to find the geocache, what challenges you will encounter while searching for it, and what you will discover when you find it.

Supporting exploration during the adolescent years reinforces a natural tendency to learn about the world and move closer to self-discovery. Your teenager will explore individually and with friends, but exploration should be done with you as well. Tour a museum, go for a hike, or visit another part of the city, state, or country. If possible, travel to another continent. Show your child that even for you, it is important to get out in the world and continue to learn about nature, culture, art, and other aspects of humanity. Your teen will have a more open-minded approach to life the more you promote openness to new experiences, ideas, forms of expression, and ways of living. Your teen will also be more likely to share new experiences with you, because she will not fear reprimand for having an explorative nature.

Encouraging your teen to explore on her own facilitates the transition from dependence to independence and interdependence. Acting independently requires courage, confidence, coping skills, and sound decision-making. Working with others requires these abilities as well as critical social skills such as listening, communicating, empathizing, mediating, negotiating, and collaborating. Encourage the innate explorer within your teen as much as possible.

Although discovery is more easily done when your child feels safe, there will be times where exploration requires stepping out of one's comfort zone. Allow your teen to do something that you normally would not. The more your child discovers at a young age with your trust and support, the less fearful of the world she will be, and the better she will navigate a world that requires tolerance and the ability to adapt.

Play

Play is so pervasive that it manifests physically, verbally, and mentally in the form of your imagination. Encourage mental play as much as physical and verbal play. Imaginative play is the fertile soil from which creative ideas sprout, allowing us to evolve individually and collectively. As Albert Einstein wisely noted, "Imagination is more important than knowledge. Knowledge is limited."

Play is not to be underestimated. It helps fulfill the need for fun, and it is an essential piece in the fulfillment of other needs. In adolescence, play is an integral part of fulfilling the need for belonging. It is a fundamental way to practice connecting with peers by observing and mimicking others. Whether one is involved in a romantic relationship or in more social realms, play is important in learning about others and finding ways to fit in. Play is an integral part of anyone's life, whether child, adolescent, or adult, and it improves our repertoire of skills for associating with others.

Play is ideal in learning conflict-resolution skills. Conflict during play is usually perceived as more serious than it actually is. The longer the parties argue, the less fun they have. By putting the conflict in the context of play, emotions cool, rationality can be restored, and an acceptable solution can be agreed upon. Arguing over whether someone broke a rule will not be catastrophic. It will not have a lasting impact on the quality of your life unless one party always feels cheated or concedes in order to maintain the play. The quarreling parties share a common interest: the fun resulting from play. This provides a key motive to come to an agreement so that the fun can continue.

Play fulfills our need for freedom with its unrestricted, unregulated spirit. Play may be bound by some rules, but creativity can alter the guidelines and give participants the courage to have new experiences. Play is an opportunity to explore talents and let loose imaginative abilities in a carefree environment. It allows you to experiment with whatever your mind, body, or soul desires, pushing your limits and offering endless opportunities to uncover your potential. The freedom of play allows you to flirt with boundaries, tempting you to see what lies just beyond your comfort zone. It beckons you to grow, learn, and be your true self.

Play also helps you fulfill your need for power as you define who you are and build upon your strengths. Play at an early age allows you to uncover your abilities and begin to carve out a niche in the world by establishing your worth in relation to others. It gives others the opportunity to see your talents and how you could add to the greater good. In larger groups where members have varying roles, play allows each person to feel worthwhile about his unique contribution and be appreciated by the group for achieving a common goal.

My oldest son once created a pencil sketch of a ninja wielding a bamboo staff, and he posted it on a social media website. He enjoyed drawing, and it was the first time he'd put his work out for the larger community to see. It was an attempt to fulfill a need for power under the guise of fun. From the immediate and overwhelming encouragement he received, he was able to appropriately satisfy his need for power. Not only had he engaged in an activity that he enjoyed, but he also felt good that others appreciated his creative abilities.

It is not farfetched to say that play is useful in satisfying the need to survive. For some, cooking dinner can be a chore. For others, it can be fun to try a new recipe, shop for unfamiliar ingredients, and prepare a meal with family or friends. Some people have hobbies outside of work while others make a living from their hobbies. Playing an instrument for a local band in the evenings or weekends might be a fun way to bring in extra cash, but some musicians make a living from it.

Play can be loosely interpreted as engaging in an activity that is pleasurable. Those who have found a way to turn what they consider play into a career have combined fun with the need to survive. You may have career aspirations for your teen; put them aside and encourage your teen to pursue a career in an area in which she has interest and ability. Even if you do not understand her career choice or think it is not lucrative enough, there is no better form of work than doing something you are interested in, are good at, and have fun doing.

Inspire

Like play, inspiration is an integral part of fulfilling needs. Inspiration takes the fulfillment of needs to a higher level that is more gratifying. What makes life fascinating and diverse is the way each one of us goes about meeting our needs. Inspiration is there as a free, limitless, and contagious energy. We eat several times a day, but think of all the foods and spices that exist and the hundreds of cookbooks that show inspired ways to prepare meals. Some may see eating as a means to satisfy hunger and do not put in much effort into preparation. Others look for more nutritious and savory experiences. When inspired by something or someone, people can exceed the basic fulfillment of a need and strive to reach their full potential. Their passion results in an experience that is usually more impactful and memorable.

The need to earn a living can be influenced by inspiration. Some people work to make a living. They see it as a means to an end and do not care what they do as long as it pays the bills and allows them to buy what they need. Adding inspiration to the successful combination of skills and interests takes your career potential to another level. Having a personal mission, a life altering experience, or the motivation of a role model adds another dimension to your purpose. With inspiration, work becomes more than just another day at the office.

Inspiration can manifest with the need to belong in many ways. When enchanted by a romantic interest, you or your teen may be moved to write a heartfelt love poem (on paper scented with cologne or perfume), inviting the individual to a nice dinner (instead of sending a text message with a heart symbol asking what is for dinner). In a larger social context, your son may be inspired by a friend to join a community group, or your daughter may become a member of a grassroots organization focused on a specific cause.

Inspiration brings out your best, and you can share it with others who share similar beliefs or interests.

Being inspired can happen at any moment and can be as simple as hearing a story of achievement or watching someone do something fascinating. The morning I wrote this section on inspiration, I stopped to talk to an older neighbor who was being walked by his dog. (From the erratic wagging of the dog's tail, it appeared that the outing was either a rare treat or the dog had a history of truancy at obedience school.) We reminisced about family and sports, as his children and I were close in age. As he glowingly talked about what a terrific ice hockey goaltender one of his sons was, his countenance suddenly changed from joy to sadness. He expressed regret for stopping his son from playing due to the excessive time and resources the sport demanded and shared a story about a college game they had gone to the night before one of his son's games. He said, "One goalie was so amazing that the next day, my son played the game of his life." His son later told him that his remarkable performance was attributed to being inspired by the agility and quickness of the goalie he had watched the night before.

Stories of inspiration exist everywhere, highlighting its frequency and importance in day-to-day life. You can be inspired at any moment, not knowing how, when, or where it will manifest and what effect it will have on you. Just like my neighbor's son didn't know he would be inspired the night before his stellar game, I too was unaware of how I would be inspired to write this book.

In May 2012, I was in Austria, visiting my family. They had been living there for a year as a result of a decision my wife and I made for her to return to her home country with our boys. At a park, I met a French-Canadian photographer and youth hockey coach named Daniel Ouimet. He was taking pictures of the area with his youngest son, Olivier. At the time of the encounter I was unaware that

Olivier (who is responsible for my back cover picture) was my oldest son's schoolmate. The next day, Daniel invited me over for a coffee, and we talked about his picture book of the wine region of southern Styria. The conversation shifted from photography to writing a parenting book based upon my work, education, and the brief interaction he had seen with my sons.

I had always thought about writing a book but had never given it serious thought. I was almost taken aback by the gravity of Daniel's tone and the conviction in his voice when he broached the topic. Over the next few days that conversation stirred up a dormant desire. Seeds of potential are within all of us, and this one was patiently waiting to be watered and given light so that it could sprout. Within a few hours, I had an outline, confidence, excitement, and reassuring support from my family. When I returned to the United States a week later, I began to write.

Like play, inspiration knows no boundaries, and its impact on a person or a group is limitless. Inspiration can come from a person, a dream, a thought, a book, a conversation, a personal experience, or nature. Being open to what inspiration can bring forth from within you will allow you to appreciate something your teen has done or said as inspirational. Seeing the potential in life, regardless of what happens, will inspire your child to do the same.

Connect

Most, if not all, of our behaviors are done for the sake of connecting with ourselves or others. The moment we leave the safe confines of the womb, connecting with a caretaker becomes a matter of life or death. As dependency decreases with age and interdependency increases, your teen has countless opportunities to discover who he is, what his purpose is, and what legacy he would like to leave.

It is important to heed your call as well, although it may not always be easy or evident. Life provides moments of clarity and self-awareness to strengthen your connection with yourself and others. Thinking there is nothing more to learn, or failing to assess your life for too long, may surface as stress, burnout, health problems, or a midlife crisis, which is likely to coincide with your teen experiencing a similar experience. How coincidental and fortunate!

The difference is that this is your teen's first time going through this self-reflective process. Your support is needed so ensure that you can differentiate between what is going on with your teen and what is going on inside you. Seek help if you are having difficulty doing so. With your backing, your teenager will be better able to listen to what is going on inside and out, be more willing to accept who she is, and show more of her true nature to others.

You do not need to have it all figured out, and you are effective only when you can give your teen your undivided attention in times of need. The more you have on your plate, the less capable you will be of remaining connected in a meaningful way. If this is the case, your teen will notice, and though your child may not tell you directly, she will put distance between the two of you. Before blaming your teen for withdrawing, consider how you are contributing to the situation. Maybe you disconnected first, and your teenager is responding to the signals you are sending.

When we look at how we fulfill our needs, it becomes clear that connecting with others is interwoven into most of our actions. You connect emotionally and psychologically with your child as a caretaker by satisfying basic needs for survival (food, clothing, and shelter). Your ability to ensure the basic necessities builds a trusting, dependable relationship with your child. As social beings, we also connect with others by belonging to a larger community. The need to belong to a group is so strong that if it is not fulfilled through basic institutions such as family, school, or other social organizations, your teen becomes prone to connecting with other young people who have insufficient or unhealthy adult connections. Relying only on peers creates an increased risk of engaging in socially unacceptable behaviors and places the entire group at risk.

This dynamic occurred with the young men I worked with who had harmful peer associations and trouble appropriately connecting with adults (as a result of a lack of appropriate adult supports). They asked why they should bother to connect with an adult at age seventeen or eighteen when they had survived mostly on their own, albeit in conflict with the law and acquiring other socially unacceptable attributes. Getting them to responsibly connect with adults sometimes required months of rehabilitation. They had to overcome years of inappropriate interactions and boundary violations and manage physical, mental, and emotional disabilities that were biological or a result of their upbringing. Having been let down too many times with abandonment, abuse, or neglect by those they needed and trusted most, they had to overcome the real dread of it happening again. To cope with the fear, they often sabotaged the relationship first before they could be hurt, only to have the unhealthy pattern repeat itself.

Connecting is incorporated into the fulfillment of the need for freedom. From middle school through undergraduate school, your teen will encounter diverse student populations. You will see a strong sense of individualism and a strong group sense simultaneously emerge in the form of cliques, teams, clubs, or organizations. Your teen will test the limits of individual and collective freedom for the sake of trying to connect with his inner self and gaining the acceptance of others.

The need for fun can have elements of wanting to connect with both the self and others. Leisure activities can bring out our creative, inquisitive sides. Through fun and play, we make discoveries about ourselves and try out new skills. Both the mind and body are engaged in learning when we play. Although a fun activity can be done alone, it is more common to have fun with others. In some cases, what is considered fun is not the activity but being with people you enjoy.

What You Can Learn from How Your Teenager Explores, Plays, Inspires, and Connects

Your teenager displays mastery in exploring, playing, seeking inspiration, and connecting as these tendencies define the adolescent spirit. These growth and learning traits are tempered only by fear or inhibition. Encourage the benefits of allowing the four components to manifest. Anyone or anything can trigger the desire to explore, leading to discoveries that set the stage for an epic journey.

Therein lies the challenge and learning opportunity. Can you relinquish control and trust your teen as he explores, plays, becomes inspired, and connects? Can you adopt such a model of living for yourself? When your teen leaves the confines of your home, he will make discoveries about himself or the world. How often can you say that? When you leave your home, how often is it to do something other than what you have done hundreds of times such as going to work, running errands, or taxiing your teen? What could you do to step into the unknown and test your confidence, courage, and ability to withstand criticism? What impact would it have on your development?

When the daily routine becomes stale, new experiences rejuvenate your life. Sometimes life forces you to start something new without your consent, and this requires an explorative mind-set. Maybe you have been laid off from the company you had been with for fifteen years and are researching resume formats and practicing mock interviews as you search for a job. Maybe a long-term relationship has ended, and you are dating for the first time since your young adult years. Welcome back those feelings. You may feel jittery, fearful of embarking on a new journey, but there is no need to panic. You have your teen to consult with, and she can provide tips on what outfit to wear for a date or an interview. There is no one better to support you than your teen.

What do you see when you watch your teen play a game or play with friends? You will see a person consumed in an activity to such an extent that nothing else matters, not even your voice. Whether play is done for fun or is competitive, your teen gives 100 percent effort. Think about the last time you played with the same passion and intensity—if you are having difficulty recalling a time, you are overdue.

How often are you playing? When you are, are you intently focused on the activity, or do you find yourself thinking about work, financial obligations, appointments, errands, or time constraints? Take the time to play for fun or for competition. When you do, block out distracting thoughts as your teen does. The more you incorporate play into your life, the more learning opportunities you have to discover, be inspired, and connect with yourself and others. Think of a fun activity to do with your teen, and do it!

Your teenager seeks inspiration through friendships, music, activities, art, technology, and social media. Inspiration triggers new ideas and renewed energy. When was the last time you felt inspired to take on a new project or pursue a novel idea for personal or professional growth? How did the inspiration come about? Examine your routine and your ability to recharge and reenergize. You haven't lost the knack to be inspired, but it could be that your routine has turned mundane and lost its pizzazz. Just as easily as your teen can be inspired, so can you.

There is no secret trick that makes your teen an expert on seeking inspiration other than being open-minded and constantly in search of new experiences. Experiences can be bought by seeing a movie or purchasing something, but teens, particularly younger ones, are strapped for cash and must rely on creating experiences at little to no cost. Experiences that are self-created and require planning are more memorable and have more meaning. Short-term bliss may be achieved through attaining objects, but long-term happiness results from relationships and interactions with others. Learn from your teen, and connect more through experiences with people and less with possessions.

How can you not be amazed at the explorative nature of your adolescent? How can you not be fascinated by the energy exerted and joy received from the act of playing? How can you not wonder who or what inspires your teen and why? How can you not be interested in the social connections your teen is making on a daily basis and what your teen is receiving from and contributing to these relationships?

Adults can become stagnant when they lose sight of the importance of exploring, playing, seeking inspiration, and connecting. However, you cannot neglect these natural tendencies for too long. When going through a tough period or a midlife crisis, elements from at least one, if not all four of the EPIC model characteristics can resurface with a passion unmatched since the days of your youth. Whether traveling to a foreign destination (exploring), competing in a sporting event (playing), discovering a new source of energy through meditation, yoga, or visiting a museum (inspiration), uncovering a buried desire or talent, meeting someone new, or calling an old friend (connecting), all these activities have their roots in the spirit of adolescence.

Why do adults place less emphasis on processes that foster growth? Adults have the tendency to convince themselves that there is no more to learn, but this is not true. There is a lost but not forgotten desire to develop buried within you. Unearthing it will reinvigorate your life and keep you on the path of self-discovery. Be thankful you have your teenager as a model. Conceptualize your life as an epic journey, one to be valued and cherished, and notice the changes that occur.

Lesson 3 Highlights

How Philosophy Simplifies Parenting
- Everyone deserves wild adventures, stories of personal courage, noteworthy accomplishments, and defining moments of development.
- Determine what is and is not in your control, and focus your energy on the former.

Explore
- Encouraging exploration reinforces a natural tendency to self-actualize and learn about the world.
- The more your child is able to discover, the less fearful she will be and the greater her ability to be flexible and open minded.

Play
- Play permits you to flirt with the boundaries of your comfort zone and push your limits; it offers endless opportunities to develop and discover your talents.
- Play teaches and encourages conflict resolution, because the alternative is the end of play, and that is usually not a desired outcome.

Inspire
- Inspiration goes beyond the bare minimum of fulfilling a need, which makes it more memorable and gratifying.

- The more open (and less critical) you are, the more likely you will be to take in sources of inspiration, including something your child has done or said.

Connect
- Regardless of what need you are trying to meet, most behaviors are for the sake of connecting with yourself or others.
- Manage your personal issues to be better able to connect with your child.

What You Can Learn from How Your Teenager Explores, Plays, Inspires, and Connects
- Like your teen, you benefit most by seeking opportunities to explore, play, be inspired, and connect with yourself and others.
- Your teen is the EPIC model to follow to unearth buried abilities, leading to a life that is more in tune with who you are as a parent and person.

LESSON 4:
Redefining Boundaries and Reconsidering Consequences

Stay within boundaries to connect with others, and overstep them to connect with yourself.
                                                                Jean-Pierre Kallanian

There are no rewards or punishments—only consequences.
                                                                William Ralph Inge

Life's a Beach

Imagine that you just arrived at the beach for a weekend getaway. You open the door to the sound of squawking sea gulls and the smell of salty marsh air. As your senses rejoice, you feel the physiological changes occurring as your body relaxes and the sea breeze clears your head. As you search for the ideal spot to set up for a glorious day, your teen heads to the surf to join in the fun with other young people. As you approach the water to test the temperature, you feel the sand change from warm and soothing to cool and damp. Clearly the coastline is where the diverse worlds of land and sea meet, but it is not possible to draw a fixed line that shows where one ends and the other begins.

Now that you are an expert in identifying needs and values and applying the EPIC model, you have a deeper understanding of why the beach is so enticing. Playing in the surf satisfies the need for fun and most likely the needs for freedom, power, and belonging. Some values expressed while playing in the waves are adventure, challenge, competition, creativity, determination, risk taking, friendship, and appreciation of nature. While the teens are exploring, playing, inspiring, and connecting with themselves and others, another factor is contributing to the enjoyment other than vast amounts of moving water and an abundance of sunshine.

The romping around occurs within a boundary that is unclearly defined, natural, out of human control, and always changing. Your teen is constantly assessing what boundaries to respect and which ones to test based on confidence and ability. Gently rolling one-foot waves bring about one set of conditions and activities such as a wave-hurdling competition. Formidable six-foot swells alter the nature of the land-water boundary. Bodysurfing may now be the game of choice with your teen asking the following questions:

Confidence and Self-Esteem
How far out do I go?
How big of a wave can I handle?
What will they say if I am not as good or I stop before they do?

Skill
Can I catch the wave at the right time?
How long can I hold my breath under water?
How good is my form and technique?

Physical Condition
How much more abrasion can my skin take from the sand and stones?
How much longer can I hold off thirst/hunger?
How much longer can I go without a rest?

When boundaries are exceeded while playing in the surf, the consequences become clear, and adjustments constantly need to be made to avoid undesired effects. Going out too far, when you can no longer touch the ocean floor, results in a loss of security. Getting caught up in crisscrossing waves can send you tumbling, resulting in a loss of orientation and a nose full of salt water, reminding you of the ocean's force.

There are even unfavorable consequences for bodysurfing too well. Catching the ideal wave with perfect timing and form could strand you like a beached whale (with a bathing suit full of sand and abrasions from being sandpapered by stones as you rocket onto shore). In this case, the glory of achievement outweighs the damage. Within seconds, the burning of salt on raw skin is replaced with a rush of adrenaline and the desire to do it again. You know how good it felt when a limit was taken to the edge with great success, and you have the battle wounds to prove the victorious outcome.

Boundaries that are naturally defined (with uncertain consequences) are ideal for growth and development. This type of learning environment provides sufficient space to explore, play, inspire, and connect, and it requires little or no outside interference except an occasional check-in. It provides your teenager with continuous feedback to make on-the-fly adjustments. Allowing this process to repeat in various settings with different players and conditions provides invaluable opportunities to test limits, develop skills, make discoveries, and build confidence. All these contribute to your teen's development and identity.

Anxiety Disguised as Defiance

One of the biggest lessons I've learned from working with adolescents and being a father is that what you see is not always what you get. Defiant behavior is not always in protest to some limit set by you or society. What you are labeling as defiance could be fear or anxiety manifesting as noncompliance. To avoid creating problems where none existed, consider what could be underneath. The outwardly defiant behavior is an opportunity to learn something valuable about your teen, so respond first in a manner that shows understanding. Your teen knows that you can enforce any rule at any time, and not all noncompliant behavior is a direct challenge to your authority.

I frequently witnessed staff members or parents disciplining defiant behavior when other issues were the problem. One teen was struggling to deal with an upcoming court date, another was struggling with a learning disability, and a third hadn't spoken to his mother in four days and was concerned that she may have had a drug relapse. The examples are endless. If your teen cannot appropriately cope with a situation and ask for help, he could show signs of anxiety or frustration through defiant behavior.

Figuring out exactly what your teenager is having difficulty with may not be as easy as you think. Let's say that your teen is doing reasonably well academically but suddenly struggling to maintain passing grades. You may start lecturing on the importance of school performance and suspend some privileges when there may be something else going on. Your direct approach may even distance you, because your teen feels that you do not understand and are out to get her.

Point out the change as an observation. You can say, "I've noticed over the last few weeks that your test grades have been slipping, and you don't appear to be as focused. How is everything going?" Your teen may tell you about some significant issue. Even if your teen doesn't open up, you have addressed a concerning behavior by starting from a point of understanding, not confrontation. Maybe the behavior will stop because you made your teen aware of it. Maybe it will lessen because, through question and discussion, you identify an underlying issue that your teen can now address.

Redefining Boundaries and Reconsidering Consequences | 65

To improve understanding, determine which needs are driving the behaviors and which values influence how your teen satisfies those needs. The youth with whom I worked appreciated this interaction, because they were not used to anybody listening to them. How well do you listen to your teen? With this understanding approach, their anxiety diminished, and the relationship strengthened. Over time, the defiant behavior subsided, and instead of acting out to seek attention, they were more likely to ask for help and share what was going on. Limit testing continued, but it began to occur for more age-appropriate reasons (such as learning skills and fulfilling needs and values), not as an inappropriate response to stress.

Here is a scenario where a teen is confronted for being standoffish to the point of disrespect. The parent treats the issue only as defiance and takes an authoritative, punitive approach. Let's see how it goes. The parent is in the kitchen, and the teen walks in.

> Teen: Hi.
> *Parent: We need to talk. You've been very rude and standoffish with me lately, and it will no longer be accepted. It needs to stop now!*[29]
> Teen: What are you talking about?[30]
> *Parent: Exactly that!*[31]
> Teen: Exactly what? What's your problem? I'm doing my own thing, and you're causing more problems, making matters worse![32]
> *Parent: You see—this is what I mean. You think you can talk to me however you want. Your level of respect for me is next to nothing. Starting this instant, every time you treat me disrespectfully, there will be a significant consequence.*[33]

---

29 The parent does not acknowledge the child and aggressively addresses the issue.
30 The teen is taken aback by the unexpected confrontation and asks for clarification.
31 The teen's clarifying question is perceived as a direct attack, further escalating the situation.
32 The best defense is a strong offense, so the teen aggressively counterattacks.
33 The parent further escalates and threatens with a severe consequence.

> Teen: You're crazy! You say I've been rude? Have a look in the mirror![34]
>> Parent: That's it. You're grounded![35]
> Teen, *storming out*: Whatever!

You don't need to be a family therapist to see the impact of the self-centered disciplinarian approach. The interesting part of this dialogue is that the teen gave the parent an opportunity to make the conversation more productive. The comment "you're causing more problems, making matters worse" suggests that there are other issues the parent is most likely unaware of.

Below you demonstrate a more productive and healthy approach. In spite of your heightened emotional state, you hear what your teen says and purposefully shift the focus of the conversation to your teen's needs. You do so by reminding yourself that the end goal is to address the concern while remaining supportive and not having the issue come at the expense of the relationship.

> Teen: Hi.
>> *You: We need to talk because you've been very rude and standoffish with me lately, and it will no longer be accepted. It needs to stop now.*
> Teen: What are you talking about?
>> *You: Exactly that!*
> Teen: Exactly what? What's your problem? I'm doing my own thing, and you're causing more problems, making matters worse!
>> *You: Why, what's going on? What other problems are there?*[36]

---

34 Feeling wrongly accused, the teen escalates and makes an inappropriate comment.
35 Creating a self-fulfilling prophecy, the parent confirms the allegation, justifying the consequence.
36 This is the turning point. You shift from disciplinarian to concerned parent. You can still address the rudeness, but your priority is to help your teen by listening and moving the conversation forward.

Redefining Boundaries and Reconsidering Consequences

Teen: I don't have time to break down my life to you, nor do I want to!³⁷

*You: I understand that you don't want to tell me your entire life story, but if there are issues you are struggling with, I am here to listen and help if I can.*³⁸

Teen: You wouldn't understand anyway. I need to go.³⁹

*You: It sounds like there are things we can definitely talk about. Let's talk later. When will you be back?*⁴⁰

Teen: Around five o'clock.

*You: What about grabbing a bite to eat at the pizzeria at five thirty?*⁴¹

Teen: Listen, you don't need to worry about me. Just give me some space, and stop nagging about little things.⁴²

*You: Okay, I'd like to hear more about how I can be helpful. Are we on for five thirty?*⁴³

Teen: I guess.⁴⁴

*You: Is that a yes?*⁴⁵

Teen: Yeah.⁴⁶

*You: Great, looking forward to it. I'm sorry for coming off harsh earlier.*⁴⁷

---

37 Your teen is still bitter from your initial response but verifies that other things are going on.

38 You reiterate your teen's sentiments, again following your teen's lead, and kindly offer an ear and a helping hand.

39 Your teen brushes you off by questioning your ability to understand but does not refuse your offer.

40 You acknowledge that there is something on your teen's mind and make yourself available.

41 A neutral environment reduces the likelihood of a power struggle. Focus on sharing common needs, interests, or values to lower defenses, making it easier to connect. Doing so over a pizza is a good place to start.

42 Still testing your level of commitment but not refusing your help, your teen provides some information.

43 You show openness to listen with the goal of agreeing on a time to continue the discussion.

44 Your persistence pays off.

45 You emphasize the value of commitment toward the relationship by politely requesting a clearer answer.

46 Congratulations! You have a verbal commitment, a sign toward progress.

47 You show your enthusiasm and lead by example by apologizing for your emotional start to the conversation.

Teen: Don't worry. I'm used to it.[48]

You choose how to respond when your teen crosses a line. If a behavior strikes such a chord within you, bring the focus back to yourself and ask why. What need does it challenge? What value of yours does it question? Once the "rude and standoffish" behavior was no longer the topic, emotions lowered, and you discovered relevant information. Later on, while eating pizza, you discover that the "rude and standoffish" behavior was not out of defiance but rather anxiety and difficulties in satisfying other needs.

Tips for Setting Limits and Determining Consequences

With the amount of limits imposed by societal structures, adding extra ones may hinder your teen's ability to handle those already in place. Boundaries should be flexible enough to fulfill needs, express values, and carry out the EPIC model. Before adding boundaries, ask these questions. Do natural or societal boundaries already address your concern? If they do, what other need or value requires support, or is it an irrational fear? Will the limit help or hinder your teen's development?

Safety can be a way to justify restricting your teen's freedom. Although the risk of accidents can be minimized, it can never be completely eliminated, regardless of the precautionary measures taken. Injury from competitive sports while wearing protective gear, harm to the psyche from a failed exam in spite of hours of preparation, and a broken heart at the breakup of a romantic relationship can all serve as valuable lessons from a life that offers no guarantees. The tendency to self-actualize cannot be repressed for too long before it comes out as defiance and spiteful acts. These

---

[48] Though a little tongue in cheek, this response shows movement toward forgiveness and reconciliation. If these tirades happen more often than you think, reflect on this feedback.

could result in outcomes or injuries that are far less desired and far more severe than what may have happened had you given your teen freedom.

Executive decisions with clear limits and no room to negotiate are necessary in cases where safety is a real concern, but limit setting should not occur for the sake of exerting control over your teenager. Doing so will only undermine the relationship. Negative consequences alone will not deter your teen from breaking rules, especially if the immediate gains of crossing a line outweigh the possibility of adverse consequences.

A boundary that takes into consideration your teen's needs and values is more likely to be followed, because it will not be seen as an authoritative way to restrict freedoms. Taking this collaborative approach helps to create limits that are simple, reasonable, and enforceable. You can simplify rules by encouraging your teen to set them. Handing over this responsibility satisfies your teen's need for power, belonging, and freedom. It may satisfy needs for fun and support values of accountability, self-direction, and trust. This respects the EPIC model and increases compliance as your teen learns to self-regulate.

Before setting a limit, determine if you are willing to enforce it when crossed. Without enforcement, the limit is nothing more than lip service. Keep this in mind when determining consequences or adding rules, because the more you have, the more you will have to enforce. To maintain your credibility and parental effectiveness, eliminate boundaries that are unreasonable, complicated, and not enforceable. They create unwanted opportunities for power struggles, and you run the risk of undermining the remaining rules. Once your teen grasps that not all limits are important, he will gladly take the initiative to choose which ones to follow.

Consequences should also be simple, reasonable, and enforceable. If needed, have them coincide with a natural consequence if there is one. If the boundary is with homework not getting done (because of too much free time with friends and not enough time studying), examine your teen's peer interactions. If schoolwork isn't getting done because of phone and Internet use, start with a discussion about screen time. Natural consequences are also effective in that they can have a domino effect. For example, excessive lateness at work results in your teen getting fired. Having no job means no income; having no income results in the inability to pay for car insurance, gas, and car payments; having no car restricts your teen's freedom and movement, and so on. If you agreed that maintaining a job was a condition of having other freedoms, this can be used as motivation to find another job.

The duration of consequences should also be reasonable and appropriate to the issue. Consequences should encourage learning and problem solving. If the consequence doesn't relate to the boundary, it loses meaning and could have your teen wondering about your motives. Let's say that your teen is fired on Tuesday for excessive lateness, and she bought tickets to a concert on Friday night. Do you allow her to go to the concert when the tickets were bought before she lost her job? If not, what is the connection? What point are you trying to make?

If you find yourself repeatedly imposing consequences for the same violation, reassess whether the limit is reasonable before concluding that your teen is defiant. For example, say that you set an eight o'clock weeknight curfew, but your teen comes home at eight thirty on Tuesdays and Thursdays. You intend to reduce the curfew due to regular noncompliance, but after taking the time to listen to your teen's reason, you discover a natural limit that needs no additional support and instead you extend curfew to eight thirty.

The youth center your teen goes to on Tuesdays and Thursdays closes at eight o'clock, at which point all his friends go home. The eight thirty curfew modification is reasonable, simple, and easily

Redefining Boundaries and Reconsidering Consequences | 71

enforceable. It takes fifteen minutes to get home, and you give fifteen minutes of wiggle room, adding a rule that he must call by quarter past eight if he is going to be late. Try it out for two weeks. It most likely will address the issue and if not, you can always reassess.

Here is another example of dealing with a simple, reasonable, and enforceable rule. It is an early Saturday afternoon, and your teen comes over to talk to you.

> Teen: I need the keys to the car.
> *You: Where would you like to go?*[49]
> Teen: I'm going to Alex's house and then maybe seeing a movie.
> *You: It's nice that you are taking the initiative and organizing activities with friends, but did you ask me if I would need the car today?*[50]
> Teen: No. Can I use the car?
> *You: I didn't have any plans. I also don't know how long you would need the car.*[51]
> Teen: I'll be back by six o'clock. Alex needs to be home by six.
> *You: Great. Saturday is typically family dinner night, and we are eating at six thirty. We've gotten away from that tradition, and I would like to start it again tonight.*[52]
> Teen: Okay. See you later.
> *You: Please remember to ask to use the car before you make plans with friends.*[53]

---

[49] Phrasing the question this way implies your approval is still needed versus asking, "Where are you going?"

[50] You acknowledge your teen's effort to fulfill a need and avoid a power struggle by letting her answer the rhetorical question. This is more impactful, as your teen takes on the responsibility to self-analyze.

[51] Again, you note that little information was given and do so in a nonconfrontational way.

[52] You use this natural curfew to bring back family dinner night, satisfying commonly held needs and values.

[53] You calmly reiterate the agreed-upon rule.

Teen: Sorry, I forgot.[54]

Lines Are Sometimes Meant to Be Crossed

Your teen will engage in activities that you consider risky. Your teen's adventurous spirit allows him to try new things and formulate his perception of the world. He will test physical limits through competition with peers in acts of bravery, physical strength, skill, and endurance. The more spirited the event is, the greater the risk your teen may take to measure up. Risk taking also comes in the form of physical expression through simple changes (such as clothing styles and haircuts) to more extreme and permanent changes (such as piercings and tattoos).

Your teen will engage in emotional risk taking such as asking someone out. Some close friendships can be as emotionally risky and unpredictable as romantic relationships, swinging from acceptance to rejection. Teens can be best friends one day and enemies the next. Anxiety and strong emotions around peers and life events can result in extreme levels of risk taking. For example, your child may do something drastic to get back at someone who did something hurtful or engage in a risky activity for the sake of winning the approval of peers. Adolescents, like adults, can play vicious mind games with each other, communicate hurtful things, or spread malicious rumors.

Attempts to defy limits happen for numerous reasons: for entertainment, to accept a dare, or to achieve a personal goal. Some transgressions occur accidentally. An outstanding academic achievement, athletic performance, or exceptional mastery with a skill or musical instrument can result in public recognition or

---

[54] The sincerity of the apology can be determined by how it was said and by your teen's future compliance.

financial reward. Some attempts to exceed or break limits can result in discoveries that benefit many.

On October 9, 2012, in Swat Valley, Pakistan, fifteen-year-old Malala Yousafzai was shot and two of her friends were injured while they were on a school bus. The planned assassination was punishment for crossing a line drawn by the Taliban that banned education for girls. Malala and her father spoke out against this unjust boundary, and she was not dissuaded by the potential life-and-death consequence for doing so. Her determination to publicly advocate for female education began years earlier, and she was nationally and internationally recognized prior to the assassination attempt. Her miraculous recovery and reaction to the use of deadly force on her for advocating for girls' education resulted in the passage of a bill that promoted free public education for all children in Pakistan. The incident resulted in nearly one and half million people signing a petition that called upon world leaders to lower the number of children without access to school to zero by the end of 2015.

People like Malala, who believe in the potential benefits of their actions, will cross lines and take extreme risks, including putting their life on the line. Think of the risks taken by pioneers, the avant-garde, or any innovator. When thinking about your teen's limit testing, stereotypical values such as defiance, stubbornness, impulsiveness, and selfishness come to mind, but there is more to it than that. How many needs are fulfilled by those who envision the advantages of crossing lines in their field or in their personal lives? In most cases, it is more than one. What values do people express by taking such action? How is the EPIC model manifested when a line is crossed?

The following chart shows what Malala's decision to stand up for girls' education might look like by examining her needs, values, and use of the EPIC model as well as the rules that guided her.

Needs	**Survival**: Although she knew she was putting her life at risk, Malala believed that education was vital to her ability to provide a sustainable life for herself. **Belonging**: Access to education is a basic human right. **Power**: Malala educated herself (self-worth) and advocated for the millions of children who did not have equal access to education (worth to others). **Freedom**: Education gave Malala the freedom to learn about the world and herself. **Fun**: Malala derived great pleasure from learning and being with friends at school.
Values	Education, learning, community, justice, equality, peace, courage, perseverance, forgiveness, determination, leadership, responsibility, risk taking, and service.
EPIC Model	**Explore**: She explored the importance of girls' education through dialogue and social media with friends, family, and community (regional, national, and international). **Play**: She enjoyed school, advocating on behalf of others, and reaching out to them. **Inspire**: Her father inspired her, and she inspired millions to join her in her cause. **Connect**: She connected with a passion within herself and with children and adults worldwide who believed in what she stood for.
Rules	Advocate for educational reform. Speak up against social injustices. Forgive those who wish to prevent human rights.

Your teenager's focus is figuring out her lot in life and answering the questions: Who am I? What do I want to become? How do I fit in? What am I good at? Your teen has much to offer and requires encouragement in reaching her full potential. Your support becomes even more crucial if your teen is different in some way from the mainstream, because this could lead to rejection, exclusion, mockery, and bullying. Knowing that you are in her corner will ease your teen's mind and help her remain confident and secure through difficult times of self-discovery.

Those who dare to cross social or personal lines and enter uncharted territory are often a crafty bunch, and they can sometimes be dismissed as crazy or misunderstood—just ask your teen. There is something to appreciate in those who, like your teenager, regularly challenge the status quo, even though such behavior may be seen as incomprehensible or bothersome. The difference between how you think your teen should be and how he actually is will be proportional to the difficulty you have in accepting his limit-testing behavior. The better you accept your teen for who he is, the better you will handle yourself when lines are crossed. Improve the relationship by helping your teen cross lines and test limits that support his nature by reinforcing and creating boundaries that can be played with for the purpose of growth.

Managing Conflict When Enforcing Limits

Interactions can turn unpleasant when emotions are allowed to control reactions, as we saw with the confrontation about being rude and standoffish. At times, your high emotional state and that of your teen can come together in unfavorable ways. A long day at work, an argument with a partner, or an unfortunate occurrence can all add to your plate of responsibilities and stress, making you more susceptible to being triggered by your teen's words or actions.

Even if you have a firm hold of your emotional state, conflict can still arise. Tension is not the issue, because it naturally occurs in relationships. How you resolve it is more important. Accepting differences of opinion and depersonalizing your teen's actions is not always easy, but these steps are necessary to maintain emotional and rational control. Your teen may be struggling with differentiating self from others and accepting what is her responsibility, or she may be trying to manage other personal issues.

You will sometimes have to make a tough decision that does not feel loving. It may put you in an unfavorable light, but you know it is right. These uncomfortable interactions need to occur, and difficult choices need to be made, especially when you feel a particular line has been more than crossed. It is easier in the moment to say yes to something you do not agree with or turn a blind eye to an issue you know will get messy if addressed. In the short run, such decisions make life easier, but they create undesirable long-term consequences (being considered a pushover and someone not to be respected, diminishing your effectiveness as a parent and your self-worth as an individual).

Denying a request does not result in instant gratification, and it could translate into an unpleasant conversation or display of behaviors. The sooner you deal with reactive and defensive responses, the better, because your teen will learn your limits too. When you find yourself having to respond to a battery of why questions, follow these simple tips. If the purpose of the questions is to seek information, answer the questions rather than saying, "Because I told you so!" or "Because I am the parent, that's why!" These responses lead to power struggles, taking the focus off the issue at hand, personalizing it, and damaging the relationship.

If the questions challenge your authority, immediately address them as inappropriate, bring the focus back to the issue at hand by restating the limit or boundary, and avoid the power struggle your teen would prefer to have instead of being held accountable. Keep the limit and consequence simple, reasonable, and enforceable. Provide consequences for following and not abiding by the limit. Sell the desired option with appealing consequences, and pitch the alternative as undesirably as possible.

Let's revisit the car-borrowing dialogue with a more aggressive response from your teen and see how you can avoid the power struggle and keep the issue on topic.

> Teen: I need the keys to the car.
> *You: Where would you like to go?*
> Teen: I'm going out.
> *You: Yes, but I want to know where you would like to go.*
> Teen: I'm going to Alex's house.
> *You: It's nice that you are taking the initiative and organizing activities with friends, but did you ask me if I would need the car today?*
> Teen: No. Can I use the car?
> *You: I didn't have any plans. I also don't know how long you would need the car.*
> Teen: What does it matter? You just said you weren't going to use it today anyway.[55]
> *You: I don't appreciate how you are talking. You know you need to ask me before making plans. Because I am responsible for the car, I need information about its use.*[56]
> Teen: Alex needs to be home by six, but I wanted to go see Jamie afterward.

---

[55] This is a direct challenge and most likely contradicts established family values and rules.

[56] You immediately and appropriately address the inappropriate comment and bring the discussion back to the issue at hand. You hold the limit and reinforce what is expected.

You: It is Saturday, and I would like to have a family dinner. We have gotten away from that tradition, and I would like to start it again tonight.

Teen: *Can't we start it next Saturday?*[57]

You: No, I want to start it tonight.[58]

Teen, *sighing loudly.*

You: Listen, you still do not have permission to use the car, and now it seems you have an issue with dinner. You may want to think about your approach and attitude. (Pausing to allow for reflection) You have two choices. You can go see Alex and not Jamie, or you stay home. Either way, dinner is at six thirty.[59]

Teen: *Seriously?*[60]

You: Seriously. It is simple. The choice is yours.[61]

Teen, *standing there humbled.*

You: While you are deciding, is there anything else you would like to tell me?[62]

Teen: *Um, I don't know.*

You: You have nothing to say about how you handled yourself just now?

Teen: *Sorry.*

You: Why exactly are you apologizing?

Teen: *For being rude and disrespectful to you.*

You: Apology accepted.[63]

---

57 This question could be seen as challenging, but you address it as information seeking.
58 You calmly hold firm and answer the question.
59 You help your teen refocus by reviewing the conversation. You give two clear choices, making one highly desirable, and you avoid a power struggle by putting the responsibility on your teen to decide.
60 The earlier sigh and this comment are minor challenges to your limit setting.
61 Power struggle averted.
62 You indirectly imply the values of respect and responsibility and the rule of making an apology when needed.
63 This is a second teaching moment to have your teen take responsibility with conviction and ownership.

Redefining Boundaries and Reconsidering Consequences

(If silence occurs, allow it, because it gives both of you time to reflect and calm down.)

You: So have you made your decision?
Teen: Yeah. I'm going to Alex's house.
You: Okay, and what time can I expect you home?[64]
Teen: Six thirty.
You: Great, see you then. Have fun, and drive safely.
Teen: Yep.
You: Looking forward to hearing about your time with Alex. I also want to hear about how you are going to approach this situation differently next time.[65]

This was a fine example of not personalizing the situation, steadfastly maintaining reasonable limits, remaining interested in your teen's life, and teaching your teen to make repairs and better express and negotiate her needs. As importantly, you avoided a power struggle. How did you do it?

✓ Did you say no?
No. You restated boundaries, values, and needs when appropriate. Repeating yourself may be tedious, but it is better than entering into a power struggle. You even coached your teen by having her examine her approach, teaching self-reflection, which is a great life skill.

✓ Did you tell your teen what to do?
No. You offered advice and gave options and consequences for each, which is highly recommended. This approach can also be used in other situations. Recall Lesson 2, when you asked

---

64 This question gets your teen to verbally tell you the agreed upon limit. You now have her word.
65 This statement helps your teen be more responsible and tells her that the relationship is important and valued.

for help with dinner preparation and gave options to chop vegetables or set the table. This way you are not giving an order but having your teen decide. Include your teen in the formulation of solutions: "I am preparing dinner. What can you do to help?"

✓ Did you tell your teen what to say?
No. With some coaching, you let your teen figure it out. This approach teaches responsibility and keeps the focus on your teen. It is likely that the sour attitude your teenager displayed had nothing to do with you; therefore, there is no reason to add comments that create problems where none existed. At dinner you can ask if there was anything else going on that contributed to her attitude.

What You Can Learn from How Your Teenager Redefines Boundaries and Reconsiders Consequences

That which agitates you the most—like when your teen questions, challenges, or refuses to follow a limit—is a gold mine for you to learn. Because your teen lives to ride boundaries, cross limits, and break rules, you will be brought along for the ride. You can resist and miss the journey or buckle up and enjoy. Let's break down the conversation to see what you learned as a parent and as a person.

- Did you feel in control of your emotions? Maybe you didn't initially when your teen challenged you and gave some attitude, but by differentiating between your emotions and your teen's, you were able to do so.
- Did you enjoy the dialogue? Probably not at the beginning, but as you continued to keep the conversation on task, you built confidence as you practiced new skills. You were

Redefining Boundaries and Reconsidering Consequences | 81

effective in moving your teen forward and caring for the relationship, and you felt proud in having accomplished that.
- Was it eventful? Yes, and you handled the bumps well.
- Were your boundaries clear? Yes, and they respected the EPIC model. You focused on the process with clear guidelines of what was acceptable and what was not.
- At any point did you feel like you were losing control? Perhaps at the beginning, but by being mindful and depersonalizing your teen's energy, you calmly directed it back to her.

Whom can you thank for the following?
➤ Having endless chances to sharpen your parenting skills
➤ Reminding you how to responsibly satisfy your needs
➤ Reexamining your values and using the EPIC model to develop yourself
➤ Examining and reinforcing rules and gestures that preserve the relationship
➤ Riding on the edge of physical, mental and emotional limits for the purpose of developing

Who else? Your teenager!

There is a poignant scene in the 1989 movie *Parenthood* where Steve Martin (Gil) and Mary Steenburgen (Karen), are debating whether to have a fourth child. Gil is only focusing on what can go wrong. In comes Gil's elderly and senile grandmother, played by Helen Shaw, who tells a story. "You know, when I was nineteen, Grandpa took me on a roller coaster. Up, down, up, down—oh, what a ride." Thinking she is having a senior moment, Gil, with a forced smile, sarcastically interrupts her with, "What a great story." Oblivious to Gil's snide comment, she happily continues. "I always wanted to go again. You know, it was just interesting to me that a ride could make me so frightened, so scared, so sick, so...so excited, and...and so thrilled altogether. Some didn't like it. They went on the merry-go-round. That just goes around, nothing. I like the roller coaster. You get more out of it."

The elderly, like the young, know the value of living on the edge and playing with limits. The elderly come to this conclusion by looking back on life, while your teen instinctively knows this. You, on the other hand, are in the thick of it, so busy trying to manage life and control what you see as your teen's challenging nature that you have neither the energy nor the desire to play with or test your boundaries. Living a merry-go-round-like life can be at the detriment of your personal development, leaving you dizzy as you succumb to the trance-like spell of the circular routine.

New thoughts, feelings, and physiological sensations naturally occur when you engage in experiences that require you to leave your comfort zone. For example, deciding to pick up windsurfing and feeling the exhilaration of gliding at high speed and the freedom of the openness around you may help you overcome a fear of open water. Your body will respond to the excitement and thrill of it all. Over time, you will become more confident as you learn to handle more challenging conditions.

All the possible consequences of trying out something new are uncertain, but what is certain is that you will somehow profit. When your teen is looking to cross a line—learning a challenging skateboarding trick or mastering a difficult dance move—the potential consequences of failure, injury, and embarrassment are always there. However, there is also skill building, new strength, and confidence. These gains help overcome the fear of stepping into the unknown. The consequence of not playing with a boundary that interests you is far less desirable than taking a chance and seeing what growth results. Just ask your teen.

Do your rules or those of society control your teen? Not really. It is his choice to follow them. Your teen will find a way to get around anything that prevents him from obtaining something he wants. If you permit yourself to be who you truly are, your nature will push you to live beyond prescribed limits, to explore, play, be inspired, and connect in ways that bring you closer to yourself and others. Denying this inclination for too long could cause dissonance within you, much in the same way that not supporting your teen's testing of limits would. Take some pointers from your teen, the expert on living on the edge. Play with boundaries and cross over some lines. I did it twice.

The first was the mutual decision in 2011 for my wife and two boys to move to Austria while I stayed in Massachusetts, working at a job that had become routine, paying for two cars and a house lived in by me and Lucy, our cat. Many thought I was crazy for letting my wife go (some thought we were separating) and even crazier for parting with my children (some thought I'd never see them again). It wasn't easy, but one thing is most certain. You wouldn't be reading this book, because being alone gave me the time and energy to write the majority of it.

After a couple years of family separation and much psychological preparation, I had a deep desire to redefine established boundaries and test limits again. My wife was willing to return to the United States due to the difficulties of being separated by an ocean, but deep down inside I knew this was not the answer. In the spring of 2013, I quit my comfortable job of twelve years[66], sold our memory-filled home, and moved to Austria. I opened myself up again to new opportunities by crossing family and societal lines using the EPIC model. The chart below shows the relationship between my decision to move to Austria and my needs and values and how the EPIC model helped in my development as a parent and person.

---

66 As much as I enjoyed my work, I needed a new challenge to further my professional and personal development.

Boundaries tested	Needs satisfied[67]	Values expressed[68]	EPIC model		
			Explore	Play	Inspire	Connect
Quit secure job with no paid job to finish writing this book	Survival Belonging Power Freedom Fun	Family Change Adventure Growth Learning Curiosity	New country, language, people, and culture	Learning new language, culture, and environment	New beginning	With other under-developed or suppressed aspects of who I am
				Trying out job possibilities	New possibilities	
Sold home to live with my mother-in-law			Ways to develop professionally and personally	Writing	Inspired by my children	With myself in new ways as a result of the significant life changes
				Reconnecting with family	Meeting new people	

[67] All five needs were fulfilled through my actions, adding greater meaning and importance to my development.
[68] The numerous values represented in my actions also added greater meaning and importance to my decision.

Redefining Boundaries and Reconsidering Consequences | 85

Moved to a foreign country		Views and role as father and husband	Doing fun activities with family	Writing	With my wife, boys, existing friends, and making new ones
	Fairness[69]		Visiting Europe	Living in a different culture	
	Diversity			Having a different lifestyle	
	Open-mindedness				
	Risk taking				
	Friendship[70]				
	Trust				
	Love				
	Responsibility[71]				
	Self-expression				
	Spirituality[72]				

---

69 My wife lived in the United States for thirteen years, and we had always wanted to try living in Austria.
70 I was looking forward to being able to interact more with my best friend, Chris, who is Austrian.
71 Finishing this book, although unpaid, was my job. Some may consider quitting a paying job (without having another lined up) as irresponsible when you have two children to support, but my immediate responsibilities at this time were to be a father and husband. I couldn't do that with the Atlantic Ocean separating us.
72 This significant and difficult change required me to trust that I was following the path I was intended to take.

Teenagers tend to live in the here and now, acting with the mindset of what can be gained by breaking a limit, not what they risk losing. They know that if the limit being broken results in breaking a societal rule, formal or informal, they must get caught in order to be punished, and their plan is to not get caught. However, if your teen gets caught, there is always the well-thought-out excuse to help avoid or minimize the consequences. Now that you better understand your teen from a needs and values perspective and know how your teen uses the EPIC model, excuses are no longer necessary. You can take this all into consideration when discussing consequences and reevaluating the boundaries in question.

Now is the time to test some boundaries, and bring forth a new interest or underused skill. Maybe you're interested in rock climbing, mountain biking, camping, starting a business, or flying in a plane for the first time. Whatever boundary you want to play with, your teen will probably be fully supportive and can even coach you, offering tips and ideas in line with your new endeavor. Who knows, your teen may even join you.

Nearing or being at the peak of your personal and professional development, you have even more reasons to spread your wings further. You may see this as a time to sit back and enjoy the fruits of your labor, ride out the last years of parenthood, and think about what retirement will look like once your child is off in the world. However, there is no better time to push the limits and see what other skills you have to offer and build upon. Why stop now when there could be more of you to develop and give to others? What's holding you back? Stop and listen. The ocean waves are calling you. It's a great day to play in the surf and try something new!

Lesson 4 Highlights

Life's a Beach
- Boundaries that are naturally defined, with natural consequences, and are always changing are ideal for learning.
- Boundaries you add should provide a framework that allows your teen to satisfy needs, express values, and carry out the EPIC model.

Anxiety Disguised as Defiance
- Before enforcing a limit, check if the seemingly defiant behavior is a maladaptive way of coping with stress or anxiety, possibly about something unrelated to the boundary.
- Depersonalizing boundary-breaking behavior and remaining calm allows you to discuss and utilize boundaries and consequences in a supportive manner.

Tips for Setting Limits and Determining Consequences
- Have limits and consequences be simple, reasonable, and enforceable, and ensure that your teen's needs and values are included in the process.
- Have your teen create limits and consequences that support the EPIC model.

Lines are Sometimes Meant to be Crossed
- Crossing lines and testing limits can benefit the group as well as the individual.

- Boundaries and limits that are most often crossed require a closer examination from the perspective of your teen's needs, values, and use of the EPIC model.

Managing Conflict When Enforcing Limits
- Answer questions that are asked to gain information or clarity, and encourage your teen to be a part of the solution versus you dictating what went wrong.
- Minimize conflict and encourage responsibility when enforcing limits by giving your teen options and consequences from which to choose.

What You Can Learn from How Your Teenager Redefines Boundaries and Reconsiders Consequences
- You enter the realm of limitless possibilities when crossing boundaries, adding breadth and depth to your life and bringing you closer to your true self.
- Look at what can be gained by crossing lines, not just which rule was disobeyed or what is at risk. There could be more at risk by not playing with a boundary.

Lesson 5:
Connecting with Your Teen

Only through our connectedness to others can we really know and enhance the self. And only through working on the self can we begin to enhance our connectedness to others.
                                        Harriet Goldhor Lerner

Building a Road to a Healthy Relationship

Just as well-constructed roads consist of layers of building materials that strengthen their overall durability, well-constructed relationships are made up of layers of supportive elements that make them long lasting. Well-built roads will not easily succumb to the extreme forces of nature and will be more resistant to the daily wear and tear from vehicles. Likewise, a relationship built on a solid foundation can better handle rough patches and withstand the occasional bump in the road.

The first phase of road construction is digging out a corridor where the road will lead, and you and your teen need to agree on a path to a shared goal. What needs do you want the relationship to help fulfill? Most if not all the needs mentioned in Lesson 1 will be included as will others that you may jointly add. Large rocks come next, and these make up the base, representing values upon which the relationship will rest. Additional values listed at the end of Lesson 2 may inspire you to think of others.

Road construction continues with a layer of smaller rocks. In terms of the progression of your relationship, the smaller rocks refer to the EPIC model, which your teen epitomizes. Exploring, playing, inspiring others, being inspired, and connecting with self and others are guiding principles. The EPIC model is self-perpetuating. It evolves with you and your teen, bringing you closer to who you are as individuals as well as to each other.

Next comes the gravel and sand that fill the gaps to hold everything in place. This equates to basic ground rules that are mutually agreed upon, simple, and reinforce your needs and values. For example, if helping others is an agreed-upon value stemming from the need to belong, a rule to support that could be offering help without having to be asked. Basic rules are different from the boundaries described in Lesson 4. Basic rules apply regardless of age or circumstances providing structure to the relationship, whereas a boundary such as curfew or permissible places to go will change with age and special conditions.

The asphalt covering is last. In a relationship, this converts to small but impactful interactions that can help smooth over a difficult journey. There will be days when you or your teen will feel trampled upon, riddled with potholes and cracks. Sometimes a simple, kind gesture can fill those gaps more quickly and effectively than words can. This can be a comforting hug, a warm smile of acknowledgment, an arm of solidarity around the shoulder, or a fragrant bouquet of flowers to engage the senses and disengage the mind and heart from worries.

Spontaneous acts of compassion can quickly improve the quality of a relationship. Everyone benefits—the person on the receiving end as well as the one who gives. When you initiate a hug, you are typically hugged in return. Think of how quickly you receive a smile when you smile at someone. Kindness is not only good for the soul; it is contagious.

The Construction of a Relationship Road

Road Construction	Relationship Construction	Example 1	Example 2
Corridor	Needs	Belonging	Power (worthwhile to others)
Large rocks	Values	Helping others	Respect
Small rocks	EPIC model	Preparing a new recipe together	Helping your teen with algebra
Gravel and sand	Basic rules	Offering assistance without being asked	Saying thank you when someone helps you
Asphalt surface	Small gestures	Your teen grabs a bowl you cannot reach	Your teen hugs you out of appreciation for helping
Overall Impact: Win-Win-Win			
You Win		You appreciate the act of kindness as a sign of helping others	You feel proud knowing you still remember high school algebra
Your Teen Wins		Your teens feels important doing what you cannot	Your teen can turn to you for help
Your Relationship Wins		Increased cooperation with meals and household duties	Commitment to further your teen's education is strengthened

Both you and your teen are responsible for constructing and maintaining a relationship that will handle foreseeable and unexpected conditions that lie ahead. Expect at times for needs to go temporarily unmet, values to be challenged, the EPIC model to be disregarded, rules to be broken, and gestures to be lacking. You travel the road together; your teen is looking for your support with the path she has chosen. Your relationship will be tested, but the parent-child journey is one of the greatest you will take. All roads lead back to you, so make it epic!

Do Today What You Wish for Tomorrow

It is natural to want to know what is going on with your teenager, but if you haven't taken the time to lay a foundation for a communicative relationship with mutually agreed-upon needs, values, ground rules, and caring gestures (and have not taken steps toward maintaining it), your desire will be met with frustration. It is unreasonable to expect that your teen will candidly talk with you or honestly answer probing questions if previous interactions haven't supported such an exchange. Think of the roads where you live. Which ones do you take? Which do you avoid? The same holds true in relationships. If your teen feels that your relationship is not well maintained and worthy of travel, he will avoid it.

You may find great advice from parenting magazines, books, and blogs, but only conscious and deliberate interactions will change the dynamic. Effort, trial and error, and patience will get you there. If you want to know what is going on today with your teen, look at how your interactions went yesterday. Likewise, if you hope that your teenager will share something with you tomorrow, be mindful of the type of interactions you are having today. What message do you send when you only become interested in your teen when there is an issue?

The quality of your relationship evolved over time and didn't start when your child turned thirteen. This explanation is too simple, and it omits a valuable contributor to the process: you. It is not too late to form a desired relationship with your teenager. A new path can always be carved out and constructed if the one you are on is not taking you where you want to go.

Start now. Improve your understanding of your teen and increase the trust between you by having regular, quality interactions that show interest and care, without criticism or confrontation. Like any skill, it requires time and practice. Make your interactions count. Ensure that they are regularly scheduled so that you can both plan for it and minimize excuses.

How much time with your teen is devoted to maintaining and strengthening the relationship? Are you looking at how you are satisfying your respective needs? Are you reexamining values and inquiring about how your teen is exploring, playing, inspiring others, being inspired, and connecting with herself and others? Are you examining the effectiveness of rules and opening up boundaries as your teenager transitions into young adulthood? Are you incorporating new gestures and routines that show that you support her development?

The quality of a relationship is not measured by the quantity of time spent in another's presence but by what you are doing when you are together. An engaging five-minute phone conversation brings more quality to the relationship than sitting in the same room with your teen for an hour while you are engaged with an electronic device. Are you focused and giving your undivided attention to what your child is doing when you are together? How does your teen know that you are paying attention to him?

Giving Attention

Giving your teen attention is not something you do only at a sporting event, school play, dance recital, birthday party, or when there is a serious matter to address. Give your full attention whenever you interact with your teen. You can do it at any time and from anywhere. A conversation does not need to be deeply personal or philosophical. Go to a museum, play a game, clean the basement, work on a project, run errands, or go for a walk. Have a conversation about the day's events, world news, relationship interests, or weekend plans. Giving attention is as simple as making eye contact when saying good morning and good night.

Ask your teen if she has a few minutes to talk. You may receive a blank look. Check in and ask a question pertaining to an interest such as what she did earlier today or plans to do later. Ask the question so it results in an account or description, not a one-word answer. When your teen returns from the movies, ask what the film was about and not just how it was. Follow up by asking what she liked or did not like about it. See how far you can take the conversation—maybe it evolves into a meaningful discussion.

If your questions are met with resistance or one-word answers, she may not be in the mood or the timing is not right. You can try again later or wait until your teen engages you. If neither of you are up for conversation, offer to do something together that interests both of you. With time and repetition, you will have longer conversations, receive more detailed answers, and find more things in common to do or talk about. When you are fully engaged, you can make a deeper connection and make new discoveries about the relationship.

It's time to put theory into practice. Stop reading here, and have a go at a meaningful interaction with your teen.

How did it go? Were you able to get a full-sentence response or even a few sentences? If you had a conversation, what did you talk about? Did the conversation grab your teen's attention, or did the conversation switch to another topic? If you ended up doing something with your teen, what did you do? How attentive were you while interacting? How did you give attention? What response did you get? What did you learn about your teenager or about yourself? What impact do you think the interaction had on your overall relationship?

If your teen is not home or busy and you think there is no need to stop reading, think again. Here is a reflective exercise to increase your level of connectivity and insight into his behaviors when you're not in your teen's presence. When you have a better idea of what your teen is experiencing, you will be more understanding the next time you inquire about her activities. You can also do this to prepare for a planned activity or conversation.

If your teen is not home, put yourself into his body. Where are you? What are you wearing? Whom are you with? What are you doing? How are you feeling? What needs are being met? What values are being promoted? Take out the value you wrote down from Lesson 2 or pick one from the list at the end of that lesson and feel what it would be like living by it while engaged in the activity. How are you exploring, playing, being inspired, inspiring others, and connecting with yourself or others? What boundaries are you playing with or possibly crossing? What strikes you the most when you put yourself in your teen's shoes?

This is training in positive empathy. Celebrate and appreciate the teenage spirit in an effort to improve the relationship and learn. It may even inspire you to engage in a similar activity! If your teen went to a concert, you might think about the last time you went to one. You can tell your teen that you were thinking about her and were looking forward to asking about the event. You may even say, "You know, earlier I was thinking about you at the concert and imagined how much fun it would be. It made me think of my last concert and how I want to go to one soon." This statement could prompt an account of the concert without having to ask!

How hard can it be to give your child your full attention or think positively about what he is doing? It may be harder than you think. In the days of blurring lines between work and private life (due to technology and greater demands at work), giving your child attention can be number three or four on your to-do list. When interacting with your teen, do that and nothing else. This requires some preparation, but such is the case with any important undertaking.

Before knocking on her bedroom door, do as you did in the last exercise. Make sure you are not physically, mentally, or emotionally engaged in something else. Clear your mind. You may have something you want to say and find your teen reading. Be patient. Ask first what the book is about, who the main characters are, or what she likes about it. If the book is part of a series, go buy it together or get it as a gift. Following your teen's lead and acknowledging her interests will have her doing the same when you get around to bringing up your issue.

Find ways to stay regularly connected to your teen through daily, weekly, and monthly activities. Family meals and preparation, household chores, family meetings, or outings are all opportunities where your teen can belong and be appreciated as a contributor to a common cause. Routine activities help build consistency and are sources of energy, security, and are a buffer against unforeseen events and challenging times.

Embracing and Supporting All Aspects of Your Teenager

If asked to describe your teen, you would most likely talk about his physical features, personality, and talents. Boasting is natural, but as wonderful as you think your child is, he most likely is not the most gifted, musical, artistic, or athletic person. That is not only expected but okay. Your teen most likely does not have the expectation of being the best at everything, so why should you? The qualities not worth bragging about are as significant and make him more like the millions of other adolescents in the world. These traits also show where you both can learn and deepen the relationship.

A natural talent or skill that is socially acceptable is much easier for you to manage. It requires support, recognition, and time to practice. If your teen does well academically and is motivated, you will have little concern about his schooling and take pleasure in talking about his scholastic achievement. If your teen is not studious and lacks motivation, your job becomes more challenging regarding his education and discussions pertaining to it. Incorporating these underdeveloped aspects into your lives will require both of you to be accepting, understanding, reflective, patient, and open to seeing the potential that lies within each one.

If you want to fully understand your teen, it is important to acknowledge her areas for growth or characteristics that have been neglected (due to mainly focusing on strengths and interests that you, family, or society deem important). As demanding as it is, it is extremely rewarding to watch your teen overcome those challenges and incorporate underdeveloped sides into her life. Your teen possesses other talents and abilities that are waiting to be developed. Giving due diligence to these areas will help your teen lead a more fulfilling life.

Some parents are aware of these hidden sides and purposely neglect them in order to avoid parting from established family traditions, social expectations, or cultural norms. This is done at the expense of the child's development. Just as your teen may avoid doing something that is not acceptable to others out of fear of being made fun of, shunned, or bullied, so to may you neglect shadow sides to avoid criticism, shame, or mockery. What if your son is skilled in sewing and fashion design or your daughter has an interest in body building, but both keep these interests secret for fear of being mocked due to gender stereotypes?

What tendencies and talents does your teen have that are not mainstream? What needs do they help fulfill? What values could put his shadow sides in a more favorable light and help him take action to develop them? Use the EPIC model to help your child gain knowledge about underdeveloped aspects and build them. Open up boundaries and limits to allow for more opportunities to foster the interest, and show support by making a kind gesture. Going through these steps can help you both be proactive when similar discoveries arise.

If you are triggered by the discovery your teen's shadow side, you may have a problem separating yourself from the issue. If you view it as a serious problem and begin to criticize or denounce the interest, your attitude will impede your teen from developing and tarnish the relationship. The stoic philosopher Epictetus said, "When you are offended at any person's fault, turn to yourself, and study your own failings. Then you will forget your anger."

It is easier to point out what you have difficulty accepting in others than it is to point out your own acceptance issues. What you notice in your teenager may be a reflection of yourself. The next time you make a comment about your child—accusing her of being impatient, for example—stop and ask yourself if you are impatient. It could be that your teen was born restless, but it could also have been learned by you or from someone close to her.

You need not be omniscient or omnipotent. Rather, be aware of who you are. Denying your shadow side could make it more difficult for your child to deal with his. You may struggle admitting your own areas of growth, but they are most likely clear to your teen and others near to you. Your teen will pick up on the incongruity between what you say and what you do if you have repressed unaddressed issues for too long.

Talking about your own hidden truths with your teen will normalize her own. Don't worry—you will not lose your status as a parent and role model. As mentioned, your teen knows you and already aware of your areas of potential growth, so acknowledge them. If anything, you will become more real than the Photoshop-enhanced person hanging on your teenager's wall. Your teen will feel less alone or inadequate, and, as important, she will know that you understand her better, because you are working through similar issues.

It is not necessary to have the same issue to show understanding. The point is that you are teaching your teen to open up. Disclosing your shadow side could even bring humor to your relationship, because your teen will start to point it out, knowing that it is no longer taboo. If you can take yourself less seriously, the times when your child calls you out can be humbling and amusing. More importantly, they serve as "aha moments" in maintaining self-awareness.

During adolescence, when the needs to belong and feel worthwhile are paramount, it does not take much for the adolescent ego to become embarrassed, shamed, or bruised. Knowing that you are there to provide support is essential in your teen's ability to overcome an obstacle or develop a shadow side. Your teen has areas of growth that are essential to his individuality. By not recognizing them, you are turning a blind eye to your teen and yourself.

A parent's role is multifaceted. You are a caretaker, teacher, coach, cheerleader, mentor, role model, disciplinarian, and nurturer. Most of all, you are human. Throughout your child's life, you will have opportunities to discover aspects of your teen that require you to have a closer look at who you are and what you represent. With that knowledge, you will gain a deeper understanding of your child and will be better able to fulfill your parental duties by creating a stronger bond with her. Along the way you will be surprised by what you learn about yourself.

Skills, Interests, and Resiliency

The more your teen does what he is good at and interested in, the more success and happiness he will derive from that undertaking, extracurricular activity, hobby, field of study, or vocational track. Being able to recognize your child's interests is important in helping him discover his passions and have the courage to persevere when overcoming challenges. As his interests and abilities align, the more competent he will become at satisfying his needs.

Parents engage children in activities at such a young age that they may not know what they are doing. It is unlikely that your four-year-old jumped on your lap and asked to go to soccer practice twice a week and play games on Saturday mornings. Until adolescence, your child likely went along with what you said and did. Now your teen may want to stop dancing or playing a sport that she has natural talent in. You may be heartbroken, having invested time and resources since early childhood to help hone her skills and adorning your home with her awards and trophies. As your teen becomes more autonomous and differentiates from you and others, her needs and wishes require your acknowledgement and support.

Encourage activities your teen has talent in, and be mindful of whose dreams you are trying to live out. Calling it quits after years of hard work can lead to discoveries in other interests. A peer or the media may have inspired a new interest, or an offshoot of what your child was already doing. If the new interest does not involve breaking any laws, encourage it, even if it is not in line with what you envisioned. Five years of piano lessons can turn into an interest in drums; seven years of soccer can turn into an interest in volleyball.

Be thankful for what was learned, not what was lost. Knowledge gained from past activities, like leadership qualities developed as a team captain, will be advantageous later on in working with others. Having made a long-term commitment alone is a valuable life lesson. In an era of point and click or touch and swipe, not everything comes easily, and your teen has learned that proficiency requires dedication, practice, and time.

You may have expectations about what your teen should study or become professionally, but what does your teen want? Be happy when he has found a direction and purpose. Let life be the judge and provide feedback as to whether what he is doing is needed or worthwhile. Your job is to be supportive, whether the pursuit is what you envisioned or not. If you are greatly bothered by what your teen is doing, your response could be a reaction to your professional happiness.

The chart below shows combinations of interests and skills and corresponding tasks for each. There are learning opportunities in each quadrant, so give each one equal attention. The term *skill* means you at least have a fair amount of knowledge and ability and can still learn.

	Interest	Little to no interest
Skill	**Box 1** Continue supporting and encourage other undertakings that fall into this or other boxes.	**Box 3** Determine how much outside forces influence the activity or if it is a shadow side.
Little to no skill	**Box 2** Find time and resources to explore and develop what may be a shadow side.	**Box 4** Is a lack of confidence or fear getting in the way? There could be something meaningful here or nothing at all.

Box 1: How much of what you do falls into Box 1? You have found a nice fit doing something that you like and are good at. Do not be quick to kick your feet up thinking there is nothing more to do. You can always improve your skills and further your interest. Interests can change over time and something you enjoyed doing and are good at may lessen because you have been doing it for so long and need to do something different. Completely abandoning an activity in Box 1 or dedicating less time to it can give you more time to apply the EPIC model to something in Box 2 or Box 3 or dig deeper, in Box 4, where hidden treasures may be discovered.

Box 2: The opportunities that exist here are endless, because your interest draws you to the activity. You can always find formal and informal ways to increase your skill level in something you want to do but haven't done yet. Through exploration and play, you may discover that you lack the ability to do the activity in a serious manner, but are inspired to do it recreationally as it is a new way to connect with yourself and others. As your teen is developing multiple skills, she could have many activities in this box. Teens use the EPIC model to develop their abilities by trying out different things. How many of your activities fall in this box? How are you using the EPIC model to develop skills in an area that you have interest? For me, writing this book fell into Box 2. I had the craving but highly doubted my ability since I had no experience. My desire to pursue this interest, after being encouraged, led me to overcome my fear. The EPIC model has been in full effect with this undertaking.

Box 3: It could be that you or your teen are doing something that you were encouraged to do by external pressures or due to natural ability, even though you have no real desire to do it. You could be doing it for financial gain, recognition, obligation, social status, or tradition. Eventually you may feel incomplete due to the lack of personal connection or intrinsic meaning. You may work for survival (in the case of paying the bills) or fulfill the need for power (feeling worthwhile to others), but does your job fulfill the need for power in the sense of feeling worthwhile to yourself? Does it fulfill the need for fun and freedom? If your teen has an overabundance of activities in this box, you may want to look at your level of involvement. Are you pushing your child in a particular direction or too involved? Is your teen a follower who has difficulty making decisions out of fear of rejection? Activities in this box can show the magnitude of outside influences on what we do. It could also be something you do like, a shadow side, but you deny it to prove yourself or someone else wrong or to avoid real or imagined negative consequences that may come with admitting to liking it.

Box 4: Look carefully before disregarding or immediately stopping something that falls into this category. You may be asking why you would use your time and resources to do something that you are neither interested in nor have much skill at. The answer is similar to that of Box 3, the difference being that you may think you are not good at the activity, when you actually are, and others think you are too. It could be a question of confidence. Lurking in Box 4 could be an interest or skill that has been denied expression. As was the case with Box 3, you may not want to admit your interest for fear of rejection or mockery, and you may refuse to do it well so that you can convince yourself and others that you have no ability at it. Developing the skills in this box will make it more difficult for you to deny them. If there is an activity in this box, ask yourself why you are not giving it your all.

All boxes contain obstacles that are self-imposed, naturally created, or put there by someone. Whatever your teen goes through, know that your child's ability to recover and adapt is greater than you think. Your teen's body and mind are still malleable. Think of your teen as freshly poured concrete—slowly conforming to the shape into which it is being poured. With coordinated effort, this form can give way to cope with challenges. Adults can be more like hardened concrete; same ingredients, but the mixture has possibly settled and hardened. Changes to your routine may not be as easy to handle, and any significant life-altering event could even cause you to crack if you are not capable of coping with it in a helpful manner.

I have seen adolescents overcome what an adult might consider insurmountable obstacles: trauma, violence, self-harm, abuse of all sorts, neglect, drug and alcohol dependency, death, learning disabilities, gender issues, pregnancy, developmental disabilities, home removals, and homelessness. I was continuously amazed at the resiliency these teens displayed when in a safe environment with the support of a few involved adults or even one reliable adult. Regardless of their history and moments of crisis, their adventurous spirit, creative problem solving, resolve, and desire to overcome awed me. Along with my own children, they inspired me to explore a strength-based model of understanding adolescents, play with a model that they use to learn about themselves and the world, and share with you an approach on how to develop as a parent (and person) by using your teen's spirit and innate tendencies.

What You Can Learn from How Your Teenager Connects with Himself and Others

Your teen wants you to understand who he is and—believe it or not—would like to have a solid relationship with you. What new ways have you found to connect with yourself and others after having looked at how your teen connects with himself, you, and others?

Your teen can help you and the relationship. There will most likely be issues (particularly critical ones that require more than experience and reason to resolve) that your teen may be better equipped than you to handle. Consult with your teenager.

An obstacle is only as difficult as you perceive it to be. If your teen is struggling to resolve an issue, look at how your feelings and behaviors could be impeding your child's ability to rise above. You may think that you are being supportive, but maybe you are being overprotective or doubtful. It could be this energy that makes it difficult for your teen to trust her ability to move forward. Deepen your connection by believing in your teenager's ability to overcome challenges. Tough phases in life require us to go beyond reason and logic and respond like adolescents by acting instinctually, going deep within ourselves.

How can you deepen your connection with yourself? How often have you postponed doing something you wanted to do or avoided a challenge that would push your limits (and result in connecting with yourself and others at a deeper level)? Put the ideas in this book into practice now. Does your teen put aside for tomorrow what is needed today? It is easy to postpone fulfilling your needs in order to help your child. Helping your teen can satisfy your need for power, and belonging (and maybe even fun), but allow time to do activities for your own sake. It is important for your teenager to see that you value your own development. Would you advise your teen to only look after others and not care for himself?

Play into your teen's interests, and formulate a plan to connect in a manner that aligns with her nature. If your teen is athletic, connect through a sport. If your teen loves the outdoors, go for a hike. If your teen is crafty, engage in a home project. If your teen is into gaming, play a role-playing game. If your teen likes to write, use electronic messaging to stay connected. You can do the same with yourself by engaging in activities that tie into your abilities and interests.

Connecting requires concentration, and you can improve this by watching your teen. In a time when giving attention to one activity is a rarity, your teen's ability to tune out external distractions can be awe inspiring. You may find yourself repeatedly calling for your teenager only to be met with silence. You conduct a search and discover him engrossed in a video game. Your child is so in "the zone" that the world could end and he would be oblivious to it. You want your teen to be focused on what he is doing (whether it is work, play, sport, or schoolwork), so don't take it personally when there is no response when you call. Should you be the exception to the rule just because you are the parent?

How more productive are you when you concentrate on one task at a time? How often do you give your full attention to one thing without being distracted? Why do you think your teen gives so much attention to something she enjoys? The more attention you give to something you enjoy, the more pleasure you derive from it. With preparation and effort, you can have the same sharp focus when interacting with your child or others.

The next time you are with your teen, make him the priority the way you have seen him concentrate on playing a video game, practicing a skill, or connecting with a friend. Clear your head and tune everything else out, just as your child is able to tune you out when he is fully immersed in an activity. Giving your undivided attention shows that you are present and that you want to understand.

Learning to accept and appreciate all your teen's characteristics requires you to do the same for yourself. To teach your teen to appreciate all of who she is, you have to appreciate all of who you are. What shadow sides have you been neglecting? What part of you has been difficult to accept? Take time to cultivate parts of you that require development. Maybe you have been thinking about exploring, playing, being inspired, and connecting with your artistic side—now is the time to sign up for that pottery class you've been thinking about. The better you know and accept yourself, the better you will know and accept your teenager.

Sometimes looking at your teen can be like looking in the mirror and reflecting on everything you may or may not want to know about yourself. The more you work on your issues, the better you can help your teen deal with his problems and not confuse the two. Being a parent is a great opportunity for reflection and self-improvement.

Every time you are triggered by what your child does, see it as an opportunity to make a discovery about yourself. Why are you having such a strong reaction to your child when you most likely have dealt with this trait in other people? Could it be that you struggle with the same issue and have yet to admit it? Does seeing it come out in your child remind you of unfinished business? Keep the analogy of poured concrete in mind when confronted with such an issue. Do not take a hardened stance with your teen. Be malleable and look at what is behind her behavior. Examine her needs, values, the EPIC model, boundaries, and gestures that are supporting the behavior.

You are always making the best choices you can to set a desired path for yourself, but there are no guarantees that your course of action will turn out exactly as planned. This does not mean that you should not set goals. Throughout life there will be events that affect you but are not due to your actions. You cannot control what happens outside of you, but you can control your response. As Epictetus stated, "It's not what happens to you but how you react to it that matters."

Resiliency is the ability to react in a way that helps you continue on your path despite what is going on around you. The elasticity of the teenage mind and spirit allows your teen to be flexible and creative in finding ways to overcome obstacles. There is no reason that you cannot take a similar approach when coping with challenges. It begins with how you frame your situation. Is it an opportunity or a problem? With the former perspective, you see what can be gained from the situation. With the latter, you see what is at stake. Your ability to overcome a challenge is also a matter of your perceived capacity to cope with what has happened as well as the availability of resources to help you achieve your result. Your teen is still building ability and confidence and may not have the same degree of resources that you have. If he can deal with undesired life events, you can certainly take control of life instead of allowing it to control you.

Lesson 5 Summary

Building a Road to a Healthy Relationship
- A relationship built upon needs, values, the EPIC model, basic rules, and kind gestures can withstand unforeseen obstacles and reactions.
- Caring gestures and random acts of kindness do not benefit only the one receiving; they also provide healing energy and gratification to the one who gives.

Do Today What You Wish for Tomorrow
- Do not expect your teen to be forthcoming if open lines of communication and quality time are not common characteristics of the relationship.
- Have regular quality interactions with your teen that show interest and are devoid of criticism, debate, and confrontation.

Giving Attention
- Giving attention does not require you to be in your teen's physical presence, but it does require you to prepare yourself, clear your mind, and focus on your child.
- Having a daily, weekly, or monthly routine to stay connected provides continuity and structure, which provides a buffer against unforeseen surprises.

Embracing and Supporting All Aspects of Your Teen
- Identifying and accepting areas of growth allow both you and your teen to become more of who you are.
- Support your teen's shadow sides by assessing needs and values, and alter boundaries to allow the EPIC model to develop areas of growth.

Skills, Interests, and Resiliency
- Encourage activities that have any combination of interests and skills, even if they are not in line with your expectations.
- Your teen is able to deal with change and challenges, provided that your support is well intended and overlaps with her needs and values.

What You Can Learn from How Your Teenager Connects with Himself and Others
- Connecting with your teen will provide insight into how you can better connect with yourself by fulfilling your needs in a mindful manner.
- Have the courage to explore your shadow side and bring out all that you are. See challenges as opportunities, and greet them with open arms.

Lesson 6:
How You Communicate

Communication works for those who work at it.
John Powell

Components of Communication

What you say is only a small part of communication; two other components make up the bulk of what you communicate. Below are three examples of telling your teen to take his feet off the table. The same words are used, but each one sends a different message based on how the words are said and your actions.

- Sitting down and putting your hand on your teen's shoulder, you look into his eyes and calmly say, "Please take your feet off the table."

- Staring at your teen from across the room, you say, "Please take your FEET [pause] off the TABLE!"

- Arms folded, standing over your child and looking down at him with a tense face, you yell, "PLEASE TAKE YOUR FEET OFF THE TABLE!"

Your facial expressions, body position, and gestures speak volumes. Your nonverbal communication sheds light on the type of conversation that will follow. The next time you confront your teen, pay attention to what your body is saying. Your facial expressions are more difficult to analyze, but if you are courageous, you can always ask your teen about them.

The last component is paraverbal communication, which is *how* you say what you say. It consists of your tone, volume, and rate of speech. Compare the three examples in terms of how the words are said. What impact does each approach have on the objective of the conversation? The three parts (words, nonverbal communication, and paraverbal communication) do not share equal weight, and your words are the least influential in trying to captivate your audience and communicate your sentiments. If you want to increase your chances of being heard, pay attention to how you say what you say and what you are doing while you say it.

Sometimes your words can contradict the message you send because of what your body language is communicating and how you are speaking. By comparing all three components, you can see how the message progressively becomes more emotional and confusing. The first example is straightforward, clear, and calm. In the second example, your teen will mostly pick up on the verbal message to put his feet down, but the added emotion shows that the focus is not solely on the command. It is hard for the teen to know exactly what is being communicated through the nonverbal and paraverbal elements. In the third example, the paraverbal and nonverbal elements detract from and conflict with the verbal message, and he may even personalize the outburst. His concern is no longer his feet, rather what's going on with you and why you are so upset. Clearly something else is going on. It is the parent's responsibility to sort out and control his emotional state, not the teenager.

Your nonverbal and paraverbal communication should be appropriate for the situation. Is it ever okay to raise your voice? If you are unable to get your teen's attention using your normal voice, then briefly raise your voice. If you are trying to make an important point, it is okay to have a more serious tone. If you need to show urgency, you might speak more rapidly than usual. Once you have his attention or have made your point, bring your tone, volume, and cadence back to normal levels.

You will occasionally raise your voice in frustration for repeatedly trying to get your teen's attention. As long as your emotional stability is within reason, there is nothing to be too concerned about other than trying to improve your reactivity, but if the second and third examples are the norm, have a closer look. When the second scenario occurs, explain your response once you have calmed down, hear your teen's side, and—if need be—apologize. If the third scenario plays out often, restructure the relationship, starting with an overhaul of needs, values, basic rules, and gesture. Consult a professional if necessary.

You can use these components of communication to check your teen's honesty. How do you know whether your child is telling you the truth when you are frequently told "I don't know" or "it wasn't me"? The words alone tell you he is innocent, so why are you having difficulty believing him? Did he make eye contact (nonverbal)? Was he hesitant (paraverbal)? Was he louder than usual (paraverbal)? Was his rate of speech faster than usual (paraverbal)? When you analyze all three components, you find that the nonverbal and paraverbal elements trump the verbal, prompting you to state, "I'm having a hard time believing what you are telling me. I believe you are not being completely honest. Let me know when you are ready to talk."

Knowledge of nonverbal and paraverbal communication will improve your ability to detect incongruences. In the previous example, you pay attention to your teen's words as well as his behaviors and manner of speech. Perhaps you are not mentally present, are withholding information, or are speaking in an atypical manner. Everyone, especially those who know you well (like your teen), can analyze the compatibility between the three components of communication and question the congruity of what you are saying. The more the three components are in alignment when you are communicating, the clearer the message becomes.

The Impact of Technology on Communication

Did you ever read an email and wonder how to interpret the message? Imagine if all communication was reduced to written words. This is not so farfetched in an age of e-mail, texts, instant messages, chats, and tweets. The incessant flow of information in text form is becoming more frequent and abbreviated, in some cases reduced to a few letters or symbols.

Nonverbal and paraverbal cues, which are essential in deciphering messages, are less prominent in everyday communication. You cannot cross-check the typed words in a text with facial expressions or body language, nor can you determine tone, cadence, or volume. You may have some inclination about paraverbal communication through the use of punctuation, capitalization, bolding, underlining, or symbols, but a written message is harder to interpret than a live conversation. A phone call allows you to gather paraverbal information from how the words are spoken, and video allows you to see facial expressions, improving the quality and level of understanding.

Your teen is out with friends and you receive a text message that reads, "Im OK home by 11." You have no visual of where your child is, you cannot confirm his location, and you have no way to know whether what you are being told matches your teen's nonverbal and paraverbal messages. You just want to make sure he is okay. Your teenager wants you to trust that he is okay, and if you have a trusting relationship, there is not much to be concerned about.

Trust becomes an issue if your teen's reporting has been misleading or inaccurate in the past. Trying to decipher nonverbal and paraverbal messages in written form is futile. It becomes even more frustrating when a text or chat with your teen becomes confrontational. If you feel that a text conversation with your teen is becoming too intense in content or emotion, postpone it until you can include at least one of the two other components of communication.

I am grateful for technology, and I used it heavily when my family was living in Austria. The Internet allowed us to see each other regularly while we were thousands of miles apart. Matters of importance always entailed the use of video. The more of the three components I had when communicating, the better I could determine their well-being. It was important for them as well to see me and read my nonverbal and paraverbal communication.

Young people today grow up with access to the world in the palm of their hands. Their relationship with technology is unprecedented. Technology makes communication between parent and child easier and more frequent, but at the expense of content and quality. The value of a five-minute in-person conversation cannot be matched by a day of text messages. There is a good chance that your teen is simultaneously engaged in another activity while texting you, further diminishing the attention given to your brief interaction.

Easy access to smartphones and other Internet-ready mobile devices makes it difficult to control what your child sees and hears. There is almost nothing you can do to protect your teen from accessing content that you deem inappropriate. One generation ago, older siblings (or older kids in the neighborhood) revealed mature content to the younger ones. The Internet has now become everybody's "older sibling" with much more information.

This stark reality necessitates the need to communicate more to help your teen process the adult content that enters faster than the developing mind can handle. Check in regularly with your teen. The next time you see your teen looking at a screen, ask questions about what she is watching or if she has any questions. The more interest you show, the more likely your teen will share with you. There will be things that your teenager will not tell you, and that is normal. Make yourself available so if the urge arises to share or ask something, your door is open. This is better than getting involved only when something is wrong.

Even though technology is reducing the need to have one-to-one conversations, it is a vital skill to develop as personal and professional interactions become more global and impactful with each generation. Any opportunity to engage your child in a face-to-face conversation will help improve his nonverbal and paraverbal skills and ability to read these communication components in others. Live conversation also allows you to be more mindful and improve your interpersonal skills with your teen.

Promoting Dialogue

Your teen does not receive praise for doing what is expected, and conversation about what your teen is doing well may fall by the wayside, giving way to what she is *not* doing well. If your teen is not doing what is expected, that means that you have to expend energy reminding, redirecting, and enforcing consequences. This can be exhausting and frustrating, causing you to doubt your effectiveness as a parent. Irresponsible behaviors need to be addressed, and there are ways to make this a conversation rather than speaking *at* your teen. Below are two conversations addressing an issue with homework. The first parent's approach does not promote dialogue. You model a more effective way of communicating in the second example.

Example A
  Parent: Do you have homework tonight?
Teen: Yes.
  Parent: Okay, so get to it! You haven't been doing a good job of getting it done. I'm tired of getting e-mails from your teachers telling me how late you are with your homework. Your grades are slipping, too, and that shows that you are not studying enough.
Teen: Yeah, I know.

The child did not need to think much about the first question, because it did not encourage dialogue but only invited a yes-or-no response. This question could also result in an "I don't know" response, which would cause the parent to become more irate. The parent's comments show urgency and frustration, but the focus is only on how the situation is affecting the parent and not how the teen is being affected or what may be contributing to the teen's inability to complete homework. How would you respond if you were the teen?

Example B
  You: What do you have to do for homework tonight?[73]

---

[73] Unlike the first example, you assume that there is homework and are more direct. This shows that you are aware.

> Teen: Um, I have biology and an English essay to write.
> You: What else do you have to study?[74]
>
> Teen: I have to study for a math quiz.
> You: How prepared are you for the math quiz?[75]
>
> Teen, *sitting down*: I know most of it and need to review a few sections I'm unclear about.
> You, *sitting down next to your teen: I have been in contact with some of your teachers, and I know you have been struggling to keep up with your homework and grades. What do you think is getting in the way of your schoolwork?*[76]
>
> Teen: I don't know. (*Silent for a moment.*) I've been having difficulty staying focused, but I'm not in the mood to talk about right now.[77]
> You: *Okay, when you are ready, I'd like to hear more. If you need help with something that is <u>unclear</u>, let me know. I'll come up in a bit to see how you are doing. Maybe you'll be more <u>in the mood</u> to talk then.*[78]
>
> Teen: Okay.

If your teen has no homework, you can ask what is being taught at the moment or if there are any upcoming quizzes or tests. In addition to generating conversation and showing interest in your teen's education, you are promoting the value of preparedness, because

---

[74] Having received some information, you inquire more, which helps your teen to remember and prioritize.

[75] Your teen's answer gives you more information, which allows you to inquire about her preparedness.

[76] By sitting down, you mirror your teen's nonverbal behavior, giving your attention in a nonconfrontational way. Your teen's answer allows you to segue into issues at school. As important, you ask her opinion.

[77] You give time to answer and learn there is something going on, but for now your teen does not care to say more.

[78] You respect your teen's request and make yourself available. The words "unclear" and "in the mood" are underlined as they are examples of verbal mirroring.

there is always something to study or review. All of your questions are open-ended, which requires your teen to think and encourages dialogue rather than a yes or no response.

The most noticeable difference between the two examples is the perspective from which the issue was conceptualized and approached. In the second, you were nonconfrontational and asked for your teen's perspective, which promoted understanding and support. It is okay for you to acknowledge how your teen's behavior affects you and others, but it is equally important for you to acknowledge how your teen's struggles are affecting him. You did both.

You went a step further by giving support with studying and offering a listening ear. Even if your teen is not ready at that moment to talk, by showing interest in what is going on in her life, you let your teenager know that you are open to listening. Allowing the conversation to be at a time that is right for her—not when *you* want it to happen—shows that you are respectful of your teen's needs.

The concept of mirroring is similar to following your teen's lead. Mirroring helps promote dialogue, because it tells the other person that you are following along. You can tell when two or more people are into a conversation by looking at how they imitate each other's verbal, nonverbal, or paraverbal communication. You provided examples of both nonverbal and verbal mirroring, which are mentioned in the footnotes. Other forms of nonverbal mirroring include crossing arms and legs or leaning forward in a chair. An example of paraverbal mirroring is increasing your volume and raising your tone in response to the other person's loud voice.

The next time your teen has a friend over, pay attention to their interaction, and watch for all three forms of mirroring. You'll be amazed at how quickly you will pick up on it. Try to notice when you are mirroring someone. When you catch yourself crossing your legs or folding your arms, see whether the person you are talking to is doing the same. The more mirroring that occurs, the more engaged you are; it's like singing along to a favorite song.

Mirroring has another benefit. If you are becoming agitated while your teen is keeping a level head, mimic your teen's cool demeanor even though you may not feel like it. If your teen is becoming upset, display a calm manner, with the hope that your teen will follow your lead. If your teen sees you maintaining composure, he is likely to do the same.

Observing how you communicate is important in gauging how a conversation is developing. In a heated debate, going from a standing position to sitting is a nonthreatening, "backing down" gesture. In response, your teen is likely to relax and mirror the behavior. Maybe your teen was standing with arms crossed, but after you sat down, her arms fell. If the arguing starts going back and forth like a tennis match, stop talking. It could take a moment for your teen to realize that you've stopped talking. She could be venting and your silence allows her to do so. You can calmly say, "I'm sitting quietly now. I'd appreciate you lowering your voice. I am listening." Her energy level may drop as she mimics your way of communicating.

The more ongoing dialogue you have, the more informed you will be. When an issue comes up, you will have an idea of what is going on based on information learned in previous conversations. The less you know about what is going on with your teen, the more you rely on your imagination. You are most likely creating a false and inflated picture and developing attitudes toward these untrue beliefs, causing unnecessary stress and panic. By assuming the worst, you are likely to respond authoritatively when you become aware of a problem.

Your last statement in the conversation is one of support; you say that you will check in later to find out what may be interfering with school and grades and offer help with homework if needed. It is possible that your teen will still not be ready to talk, but you can always check in again. Following through with what you say shows the level of importance you place on his well-being, education, and life. You also promote the values of dependability and reliability. Checking in is a caring gesture that improves the overall health of the relationship.

Not all questions need to be an attempt to see how responsible your teen is being. Inquire about your teen's favorite activities and interests. Ask thought-provoking questions such as her views on religion, politics, philosophy, art, and current events. You may be pleasantly surprised by her opinions and knowledge and will have a better understanding of how she conceptualizes the world. This information provides insight into how she goes about navigating life. Increasing the frequency of conversations that highlight competence and interests makes it easier to approach more difficult topics. More importantly, you will be the parent who genuinely cares, not the parent who gets involved only when something is wrong.

Hear What Your Teenager Has to Say

Communication entails talking and listening. How you listen and what you focus on will influence your response. Are you hearing what your teen is saying, or are you hearing what you want to hear? How can you improve your listening skills to increase comprehension and respond in a more understanding manner?

Think of the senses involved with listening. Your ears listen to the words and how they are said. Your eyes assess expressions and mannerisms. Your mouth can utter words or remain closed. Epictetus stated, "We have two ears and one mouth so that we can listen twice as much as we talk." Having two ears, two eyes, and one mouth, we should listen and observe four times more often than we speak. If it is difficult for you to not interrupt, focus on breathing through your nose with your mouth closed.

Say that it is a Saturday afternoon, and you are reading in the living room. Your teen lifelessly plops down in a chair beside you.

> You: What's the matter?
>
> Teen, *not making eye contact, barely audible*: Nothing.
>
> You, *looking at your teen*: You look down. What's going on?[79]
>
> Teen, *still not making eye contact*: I'm bored.
>
> You: You're bored. How come?[80]
>
> Teen, *making some eye contact*: There is nothing to do.
>
> You: That's strange. You usually have plans with friends on the weekend.[81]
>
> Teen, *perking up*: Yeah, well, not this weekend (*stands up and walks to the kitchen*).
>
> You, *standing up and following your teen*: What's different about this weekend?[82]
>
> Teen, *silent*.
>
> You, *silent*.[83]
>
> Teen: Alex and I had plans to do something today, but we got into a big argument two days ago, and we haven't spoken since.[84]
>
> You: Does that explain why you are bored and look like you just lost your dog?[85]

---

79 Making the observation shows that you are paying attention, and checking shows that you want to confirm it.
80 Verbal mirroring shows that you are listening, and your question shows that you want to know more.
81 Your observation shows that you pay attention to your teen's life.
82 You display nonverbal mirroring and ask an open-ended question.
83 You do not break the silence, giving your teen time to think and respond.
84 Your teen breaks the silence and tells you what is going on.
85 You ask to make sure your observation is correct and add humor to lighten up the situation.

Teen, *looking at you with a half smile*: Basically.[86]
    You, silent.
Teen: We don't fight often. It sucks because it ruined our plans for this weekend.[87]
    You: Yes, arguments sometimes happen between friends, and as you said, it doesn't happen often. Friends usually find a way to make peace and move on.[88]
Teen: Yeah, we're pretty good about not holding grudges for too long.[89]
    You: You've known each other for a long time now, so I'm sure this is not unfamiliar territory for the both of you.[90]
Teen, *after a few seconds*: It was over something stupid. In the moment, it seemed serious, but when I think about it now, it was not that important.[91]
    You, smiling: Thanks for telling me about what was bothering you. It helped me better understand where you were coming from. I am heading out to run some errands. Want to join me? Afterward we can grab a bite to eat and catch a movie.[92]
Teen: I'm not sure if I feel like it.
    You: Come on—it will be fun. Would you rather sit around here feeling miserable?[93]
Teen: Okay, give me a few minutes to get ready.

---

86 Your teen affirms your conclusion and responds positively to your humor.
87 When you allow silence, you give your teen the space to tell you more.
88 You acknowledge and normalize the issue and give words of encouragement.
89 Your encouraging words have your teen talking in a more hopeful manner.
90 You express confidence in your child's ability to move on.
91 Your calm, supportive approach helps your teen see the incident more objectively.
92 Your statement invites your teen to open up and share with you, and your invitation continues to show support.
93 You eradicate the remaining self-pity and encourage a change of scenery and focus.

Your teen might have difficulty telling you what is bothering him or only make a suggestive comment. Figuring out what your teen is saying can be detective work, requiring you to read between the lines. Your teen was moping around the house. When you asked what the matter is, the response was, "Nothing." The behaviors and words didn't match, so you had a hard time believing your child. How did you encourage your teen to share what was going on?

You gave your undivided attention by stopping what you were doing and continuously paid attention to all three forms of communication. You asked open-ended questions to promote dialogue and checked in whenever you made an observation to avoid assumptions. You used verbal and nonverbal mirroring and when you followed your teen in the kitchen, you gave him space. Because your teen needed to talk and not you, you observed and listened. You spoke calmly and in a supportive manner, creating an inviting space for your teen to open up.

You effectively harnessed the power of silence, which can often cause feelings of unease. If you learn to be comfortable with the awkwardness that silence can evoke, you can effectively use it as you did in the example above. Rather than demanding an answer, you patiently waited twice for the silence to work its magic. Without prodding, your teen opened up and began to share what was going on. Silence gave your teenager time to process the discussion, which could have triggered feelings associated with the actual incident (in this case, the disagreement with the friend). It also gave you time to process the conversation. Allowing silence helps relieve pressures associated with emotionally laden discussions.

Respecting the power of silence resulted in key interventions that helped move the conversation forward. This conversation was not about you. It was about your teen. By keeping quiet, you gave your teen the time and space to take the discussion where he wanted it to go. Once you were told about the argument with the friend, you did not immediately come to the rescue by giving advice on how to repair the relationship. You restated the problem and looked to confirm your teen's sentiments by matching his feelings with his behaviors and comments.

Restatements show your teen that you are listening and allow you to determine whether you understand the situation. If not, your teen will let you know. Showing understanding without passing judgment puts your teen at ease and encourages him to continue disclosing. By taking this approach, you can feel the conversation opening up. With less resistance on your teen's part, the conversation is no longer a guessing game or interrogation but a flowing conversation about an important adolescent topic: relationships.

You took it a step further by thanking your teen for sharing, and you offered an invitation to join you. This was a kind gesture that addressed the issue of boredom along with unmet needs such as fun, belonging, power, and freedom. When behaviors change, thoughts and feelings tend to follow, because they are all connected. This conversation had a happy ending. However, even if your teen did not accept the invitation, your gesture was supportive and said that you care about him and the relationship.

What You Can Learn from How Your Teenager Communicates

You do not depend on your child much to have your needs met. You do not need her permission to make a purchase or go somewhere. Your teen depends on you and others to help satisfy her needs.

Although it diminishes with age, the need for approval continues into late adolescence and possibly early adulthood.

With time and practice, your child will become adept at reading your mood by checking how well your nonverbal, paraverbal, and verbal responses match. This information is valuable in determining how and when to approach you to gain the support to satisfy his needs and express his values. Are you as skilled in gaining support from your partner to quit your job and travel for half a year? To obtain approval from your boss to take a leave of absence with half pay? To get your landlord's permission to sublet your apartment while you are away?

Your teenager is curious and inquisitive. She is learning to digest the world and satisfy needs through roaming eyes, scanning ears, and a calculating mind. This may be viewed as conniving and manipulative, but the ability to understand nonverbal cues and pick up on the minutiae of social behavior is extremely beneficial, especially considering that many of our interactions with others involve making a request, compromising, or negotiating. Would you pick any random time to ask someone out on a date or ask your boss for a raise? The process you use before asking these potentially life-altering questions is similar to the way your teen approaches you on matters of importance.

The young people I worked with were experts in finding creative ways to fulfill their needs, because the more traditional way—forming healthy adult relationships—was often lacking. Years of living in unpredictable environments and with erratic caretakers provided them with intense training, making them proficient in detecting subtle incongruities between verbal, nonverbal, and paraverbal communication. Like all children, they learned how to communicate through observation and trial and error. The chaotic environments taught them that in order to survive, they needed to pay close attention, sometimes on a minute-by-minute basis.

Living in unpredictable surroundings—their homes, schools, and neighborhoods—they needed to be alert and ready to respond to random events that could jeopardize their emotional, psychological, or physical safety. Because their caretakers hadn't been responsible in helping them satisfy their needs, they would look for opportunities to walk away unscathed and satisfy a neglected need in the midst of the chaos. With chaos comes opportunity, and many youths with this background thrive in the midst of chaos, because this is what they are familiar with.

Regardless of background, most teens are professional observers. Not only will they pay attention to you when you are talking with them, but if other children are around, they will pay close attention to how you interact with them. Teens will notice whether you interact with other children the same way you engage with them. If there is an advantage to be gained, your teen will make you aware of any discrepancy and even question you about the differing treatment. They pick up tips when they see a sibling or another child successfully obtain something from you, and they modify or abandon tactics that fail. How often do you observe and learn from the way others communicate?

Adults may think there is not much more to learn in life, and if there is, it most likely will not be learned from teenagers. If there is an issue with communication, many adults think the other person must be the problem. If you see your teen successfully negotiate a deal or fulfill a wish through an interaction, inquire and take notes. The next time your teen makes a request and you comply, pay attention to how she approached you. What can you take away from the interaction?

When your teen asks you for money or permission to go somewhere, he may embellish or exaggerate some details. This is an attempt to build a case and tug at your heartstrings. Another approach may be reasonable, coherent, and respectful, with justifications as to why you should agree with the proposal. The charm can be turned on when needed. Negotiation is a last resort, and your teen will become better at it. Over time, your teen will come to the negotiation table more prepared. This is beneficial, because we negotiate more often than we realize.

As an adult, you may communicate less effectively because you think you have earned the right to do what you want when you want without having to seek approval from others. You may think you need to depend less on others, but this is not entirely true. You depend on clients, coworkers, friends, family members, neighbors, and, in some cases, strangers. How would you describe your interactions with them? The next time you ask something from a friend or a colleague, pay attention to how you approach the person. How do people respond to you when you ask for their help?

You might not think you depend on your teenager as much as he depends on you, but you do. You depend on your teen to fulfill household obligations, abide by family rules, master skills, and mature. You have a mutual interest in raising a responsible, contributing member of society.

You model how to effectively communicate. You may be sensitive to how your teen communicates with others, as her actions could be a reflection of your parenting. How would you respond if your teen walked into the living room without acknowledging you and bluntly said, "Give me the keys to the car. I'm leaving." If this type of communication exists, ask if you do the same. How your teen communicates is likely similar to how you communicate. We tend to notice in others what we fail to see in ourselves. Pay more attention to how you communicate. Use your child as a sounding board to learn more about yourself.

Your image and reputation are affected by how you interact with others. How you express yourself is a large part of who you are, so much so that you recognize others by their voice, mannerisms, and tone alone. You can always improve your manner of communicating. I am proud when my children say *please* and *thank you*, and it reminds me to be courteous.

Lesson 6 Highlights

Components of Communication
- Communication is made up of verbal (words), nonverbal (facial expressions and body language), and paraverbal elements (tone, volume, and cadence).
- Nonverbal and paraverbal communication convey most of what you say. The clarity of your message improves when these elements coincide with your words.

The Impact of Technology on Communication
- Include as many of the three components of communication when using technology to communicate. Use face-to-face talks for more serious conversations and to teach interpersonal skills.
- Communicate regularly with your teen to stay informed about all that he is reading and watching on the Internet.

Promoting Dialogue
- Approach conversations from your teen's point of view, ask open-ended questions, mirror your teen (when appropriate, have your teen mirror you), and include gestures that promote respect and understanding.
- Take the time to acknowledge responsible decision making, highlight competencies and interests, and engage your teen in conversation about world views and events.

Hear What Your Teenager Has to Say
- Use your ears to detect paraverbal messages and listen for the underlying message. Use your eyes to watch for nonverbal behaviors.
- Improve your listening skills by giving your full attention, allowing silence for reflection, having your teen break the silence, being nonjudgmental, and using restatements to clarify.

What You Can Learn from How Your Teenager Communicates
- Your teen is a keen observer and a master of self-advocacy, so learn from how your teen negotiates and seeks assistance from others.
- Be as critical of your own manner of communicating as you are with your child. When you notice your child communicating in a way that you find bothersome, ask yourself whether you communicate in the same manner.

Lesson 7:
Ensuring Health and Wellness

Healthy people are those who live in healthy homes on a healthy diet, in an environment equally fit for birth, growth, work, healing, and dying.

Ivan Illich

Care for Yourself and Your Home

Parenting requires constant juggling of duties. You can become so engrossed in the minutia, trying to balance your immediate needs and those of your child that you forget about your own health and wellness. How is life impacting your teen's overall health and well-being?

Your teen's life is in transition, and so is yours. Maybe you are switching careers or making a drastic life change. In times of transition, staying in the moment can help you stay focused. Thinking too far ahead can leave you feeling overwhelmed as you envision all the projects and deadlines you are facing. There is nothing wrong with setting goals and planning ahead, but be mindful that you have control only over what is going on now. Achieving smaller tasks will bring you closer to accomplishing long-term objectives and will help you maintain your sanity.

As the parent of a teen, you are most likely in your late thirties to midfifties. Not only is your teen's body undergoing transformation, so is yours. Are you encouraging yourself to exercise as much as you encourage your teen? How regular is your fitness routine? You require continual care to remain physically and cognitively fit. You remind your teen to study, but are you actively training your brain and learning?

Putting your health first will result in a more balanced you. Even when tending to your teen's needs and forgoing some of your own, you can be mindful of your well-being. Maybe your teen is habitually late in getting to a practice or lesson, and so you make up time by driving faster than usual. Is speeding worth jeopardizing your welfare or that of your teen? By exceeding safety limits and driving with a high level of anxiety, what message are you sending? How does your risky behavior help the situation? It excuses your teen's lateness, enabling the tendency to procrastinate at the expense of your well-being and that of your child.

To change an unhealthy dynamic of your teen, you need to detach from it. You most likely have enough to deal with, so you don't need to take on those of your teenager. Help find ways to improve her wellness instead of jeopardizing it. In the situation above, you are the chauffeur. Drive safely. If you arrive late because your teen wasn't ready, so be it. If the coach or teacher asks why you are late, ask him or her to speak to your teen. Separating yourself from your teenager's behaviors and having a sound mind, body, and spirit will allow you to better handle the responsibilities of being a parent and managing your own life.

Your well-being should be taken into consideration with all you do. How can you ensure self-care when you have a tight schedule and little free time? Take a tip from your teen. Turn any situation into an opportunity to improve your well-being. Recall from the introduction that everything you need is nearby. Be present and mindful of needs and values. Apply the EPIC model. Follow simple rules, and practice basic caring and healing gestures wherever you are.

Continuing with the chauffeur analogy, unless you live in an area with reliable public transportation, one of your regular duties might be taxiing your teen. Much of your time can be waiting, because it may not make sense to drive home just to return an hour or two later to pick up your child. Instead of sitting in your car checking work e-mails and other messages, engage in an activity that contributes to your health and wellness. Research the area. Look for a park where you can walk or run. Be adventurous and explore.

Whatever you are doing, ask whether it is contributing to your health. If it is, continue. If not, reconsider. Caring for yourself is a question of how, when, where, and with whom. Put a well-being program in place by getting creative with time management, forming new habits, and collaborating with friends, neighbors, and family.

Here are two examples of how to develop a model for improving your well-being.

Road Construction	Relationship Construction	Example 1: Start Running	Example 2: Take a Cooking Class
Corridor	Needs	Survival, belonging, power, freedom, fun	Survival, belonging, power, freedom, fun
Large rocks	Values	Health, fitness, and being outdoors	Challenge, health, creativity, and mastery
Small rocks	EPIC model	Run trails (Explore); strength train (Play); run a charity race (Inspire); meet runners (Connect)	Explore ethnic cuisine, play with unusual ingredients, be inspired by cookbooks, and connect with your creative side
Gravel and sand	Basic rules	Run 3x/week, long jog 1x/week, strength train 1x/week, and eat healthier	Use local produce and each week try an unfamiliar ingredient
Asphalt surface	Small gestures	Buy running gear, run a race with your teen, and splurge on an ice-cream sundae afterwards	Buy nifty kitchen gadgets, make your teen's favorite meal, and prepare a meal with your teen

Overall Impact	Running	Cooking Class
You Win	You are more fit, energetic, and confident	Expand your culinary repertoire, learn about new ingredients, and improve your cooking
Your Teen Wins	You may inspire your teen to run, or maybe you are inspired by his athleticism	Your teen eats more meals at home, eats more nutritiously, and is inspired to cook more
Your Relationship Wins	You can run together and encourage each other to stay fit	You can spend quality time with your teen in the kitchen while preparing and eating tasty meals

By incorporating your health into your needs and value system and using the EPIC framework, you will be more mindful in everything you do. You will create new supporting guidelines and gestures. Simple rules to promote your health can be as easy as taking the stairs instead of the elevator or drinking a glass of water instead of a soda. These small decisions quickly add up, creating new habits and improving your overall wellness.

When thinking about wellness, remember your mental and emotional health. Activities such as meditation, prayer, and creative outlets for self-expression help keep you balanced cognitively, emotionally, and spiritually. Take a few deep breaths before entering a difficult meeting. The more skills and outlets you have to maintain your health, the better you will cope with life events and achieve your personal goals. Let your teen motivate you to become sound in mind, body, and spirit. Exercise with your teen, who may have fitness tips for you. Ask your teenager to join you, and feed off one another. The more you and your teen engage in routine activities that promote health and wellness, the more you encourage and inspire each other.

At times, your teen will be in environments where conditions are not ideal and over which you have no control. There is one place where you can greatly influence the setting: your home. When there are uncertainties in your teen's life, you are in charge of creating and maintaining a home where she can seek solace. All family members add to the culture and upkeep of the home, and your teen should take on more responsibility in making your home a healthy, safe place.

If he is not doing so already, your teen should contribute to household chores. Helping around the home instills a sense of responsibility and community that is important at a time in life when there is a tendency to focus on one's self. For larger projects, working side by side with your teenager provides the additional benefit of spending quality time together. It gives you the opportunity to talk about matters that are important to him without seeming as if you are intentionally prying into his life. Working together can also be an opportunity for your teen to learn a new skill or for you to learn something from him.

Personal space and privacy take on more importance during adolescence. Your teen's bedroom is a place where she can show her personality. You can learn a lot from how the room is used and kept and what objects occupy the space. What you see as clutter or disorder is often a safe haven for your teen. Other spaces in the home, including garages and attics, can be places to retreat alone or with friends. How does your home support your teen's ability to fulfill his needs?

Rooms have personalities and can have purposes other than their intended ones. Some spaces are more conducive to gatherings due to location or ambiance. Kitchen tables are used as work spaces and living rooms as gym floors. Dining rooms become associated with fond family reunions and celebrations. What personalities and purposes do rooms in your home have?

Decoration and furniture give your home character and can promote the values your family embraces. For example, in our dining room in the United States, we had art hanging on the walls that we received from friends, extended family, my children, and my wife. Artifacts brought from visitors or from our trips to other parts of the country or foreign lands were also on display. At face value, the objects are merely decorative, but the deeper message was one of family, friendship, diversity, and travel, all signifying exploration, play, inspiration, and connection.

Staying Cool When You Are Feeling Hot

Think of the last time you became angry at what your teen did or said. How did your body respond? What did you think? How did you feel? How did you handle the situation?

Regardless of what unpleasant situation you end up in with your teen, remember that your response is your choice. Just as you do not accept excuses for your teen's irresponsible behavior, you cannot blame your teen for your reaction. What can you do to remain calm if you are about to enter a confrontation with your teenager?

Let's look at what you know about creating a dynamic that is pleasant during conversations with the potential for high emotion. Background information can increase your understanding and lessen your anxiety and fear. To that end, answer as many of the following questions prior to the potentially heated discussion to detach emotionally and improve your understanding of why your teen is behaving in such a way.

Preconversation Questions
- What needs are driving your teen's behaviors? If there is a dilemma, what needs are competing?
- What values are influencing your teen's behaviors? Which of your values did your teen's behavior challenge? What values will help facilitate the discussion? What values can you incorporate into your life?
- How did the behavior help your teen explore, play, inspire others, be inspired, or connect with self and others?
- What natural and created boundaries were in question? Which ones were played with or crossed? What was the desired outcome for doing so? If necessary, how can you include your teenager in renegotiating boundaries?
- What shadow side was displayed, and how was it developed through the behavior? How did your teen show resiliency?
- What skills were practiced or interests shown?
- What decisions can you commend (or what behaviors can you highlight) that showed competency and responsibility? Ask open-ended questions to find out.
- Based on recent discussions with your teen, what other information could be applicable to the behavior or situation? How can you help your teen make these links?

Even after doing this preparation, you might still disagree with the behavior and outcome, but doing your homework permits you to look for strengths to build upon. You will have background information that will ease emotions, promote dialogue, and improve understanding. You also have tools to further understanding, keep the lines of communication open, and continue building a healthy relationship. Let's review.

Conversation Toolbox
- You know how to effectively use the three components of communication: verbal, nonverbal, and paraverbal.
- Mirror your teen's communicative style or, if necessary, have him mimic yours.
- Maximize listening by giving your full attention, rephrasing key points, asking open-ended questions, withholding judgment, allowing silence, and letting your teen break it.

The three possible outcomes to any discussion are agreement, disagreement, or indifference. No matter how well prepared (or right) you think you are, there is no guarantee of being in agreement. Is reaching an agreement always necessary?

If you can reach an agreement, congratulations! With some dialogue and negotiations, you settled on consequences, and possibly made changes together to boundaries. You may be shaking your head, asking, "When does that happen?" If there is mutual respect, understanding, and trust in the relationship, this will be a more frequent outcome. Like seasoned negotiators who meet regularly, eventually you will come to the table having a good idea what your teen will ask for and what you expect in return.

When agreement or understanding is not reached, you need to know when you both have said everything, and accept that at this time there is no agreement. In the field of negotiation, the acronym BATNA stands for Best Alternative to a Negotiated Agreement. It is better to stop with no agreement and put the conversation on hold than to make a comment that damages the relationship. Focus on the relationship and keep the lines of communication open. Make preserving the relationship your BATNA.

Like the use of silence, a complete break in a conversation can allow time to reflect. Use this time to reconsider your stance and your teenager's viewpoint. Review in greater detail your preconversation questions. Use new information to increase your understanding of the situation and ease your emotions. Neither of you wants issues to linger, particularly if other things are contingent upon the resolution.

What are the signs that a conversation is not going well? Be aware of your physiological response—your body will let you know if you are having difficulty accepting what you are hearing. Raising your voice, sweating, pacing, clenching your fists or teeth, or feeling your heart rate increase are signs to end the interaction and come back to it when you are calmer.

Pay attention to mental cues as well. Thoughts like "This child never listens," "When will my son get it?" or "My daughter is hopeless." If you start swearing in your head or having aggressive thoughts, it is definitely time to stop the conversation and walk away. If you are calm enough to say that you need a break, do so. If not, just walk away. You can always explain your departure later. Better to walk away without communicating than to stay and communicate risky thoughts. If your teen cannot calm down, suggest taking a break and tell her that you need to step away. Refer to Lesson 5 if you need some help rebuilding the relationship.

Ambivalence, or no response from your teenager can be even more difficult to handle. With refusals or outbursts, you at least have a point from which understanding can improve. Apathy can leave you guessing what your teen is thinking and feeling and have you formulating scenarios that are likely not true. You may take offense, because you are not being acknowledged. Stop before your thoughts and emotions get the best of you.

When there is conflict or ambivalence, there could be a more concerning issue that your teen needs to address before the present problem can be resolved. Recall from Lesson 4 the section on anxiety disguised as defiance. Rule out other issues by asking if there is anything else going on before continuing. You will not subdue your teenager with force. You will only give him more reason to retreat and be unresponsive. Remember your BATNA.

When you reach an impasse, shift the focus. Do something fun, and get your mind on more pleasant thoughts. Your teen most likely desires a break as well. You can go your separate ways, or you can invite your teen to join you. This shows that although you are not happy with where things stand, you are not holding a grudge. Just because you did not come to an agreement does not mean that you cannot do something fun together now that can help you reach a solution later.

Debriefing with a friend, partner, or family member can help when you are stuck. Talking with someone allows you to vent and process the event. As you discuss the situation, you can look at the effectiveness of your approach. The person may also have feedback or share a similar situation and how she handled it. If you cannot find anybody to talk to but still feel the need to talk, you can write down your thoughts.

Once you have worked through a difficult conversation with your teenager, it is helpful to talk about the process later. Focus on what helped, what went well, and what can be done to facilitate dialogue. Give your child space to share his experience. Processing after arguments improves communication, a lesson in listening and understanding.

To a certain extent, you can influence the outcome of an interaction, but there are no guarantees. Instead, develop and refine a healthy communicative process. Your overall wellness is shown through your interactions. Your individual well-being influences the shape of the relationship, and the health of your relationship influences your individual well-being. Take care of both.

Learning from Mistakes

You are happily driving and talking with your teen when you are abruptly cut off. You hit the brakes and swerve away, avoiding an accident. As the car comes to a screeching halt, you are sweating, and your heart is pounding. These are normal physiological responses to such an incident. Now that you are out of harm's way, how do you choose to respond to the situation? Do you start swearing, yelling, honking your horn, making offensive gestures, or speeding up to tailgate the driver? Do you check to make sure your teen is okay, saying how thankful you are that no one was hurt? Do you talk about the importance of defensive driving and keep the focus on you and your teen, not the other driver? Maybe you do a little of everything.

Whether you are at your best or your worst, you are always showing your child how to responsibly satisfy needs and interact with others under different and at times difficult conditions. Your attitude and behaviors when things are going well are mostly unremarkable, but the way you respond under stressful conditions is more interesting for your teen to observe.

You are as fallible as your teenager and as responsible for making repairs. Owning up to mistakes creates an opportunity for growth and learning and is healthy for the relationship. Apologizing when you have erred does not weaken your status as a parent. On the contrary, saying you're sorry shows that your title and position are not to be used without restraint or consequence. Answer the following questions before apologizing:

- Why are you apologizing?
- How will you make the apology?
- When will you make the apology?
- Where will you make the apology?

Saying you're sorry is not always easy, especially if you do not feel that you were in the wrong but someone else thinks you were. It is important to model the importance of an apology in a way that is meaningful and sincere.

Let's revisit the inappropriate response in Lesson 2 regarding the mess in the kitchen. You were having an off day and responded emotionally. Yes, it even happens to the best of us! Dinner is over, and no conversation took place. You could have handled the situation more calmly and want to turn the earlier inappropriate response into a learning opportunity. You wash the dishes to relax before apologizing. This also gives your teen time to retreat to his room to calm down. You've answered the four questions and are on your way to your teen's bedroom.

> *You, gently knocking on the door*: Can I come in?[94]
> Teen, *pausing*: Yeah.
> *You, sitting down and making eye contact*: I'm sorry for how I addressed you earlier. I was already upset from work, and when I came home and saw the counter, I snapped at you. Just

---

[94] Knocking is respectful, and asking permission to enter is a way to check if it is a good time to talk.

*like you are responsible for picking up after yourself, I am responsible for controlling my emotions.*⁹⁵

Teen: That's okay. I've noticed you've been more on edge these days.⁹⁶

*You, silent.*⁹⁷

Teen: I'm sorry for not putting the food away and cleaning up. I know I need to do a better job picking up after myself.⁹⁸

*You, putting your arm around your child and smiling: It seems that we both can do a better job at being more mindful of what we say and do.*⁹⁹

Teen, *smiling back*: I guess.¹⁰⁰

*You: So tell me about your afternoon swim.*¹⁰¹

It is important for your teen to see and hear you apologize when you are in the wrong. Likewise, your teen should know that you do not hold grudges when he is in the wrong. In this dialogue, you sent the message that you can both learn from mistakes. Being able to let go and move on shows that you value the relationship. The image of the parent as the perfect role model is both unrealistic and unattainable, but you have an obligation to continually examine your effectiveness. Use opportunities to improve your parenting skills in the same way you stay abreast of developments in your field to improve your abilities and enhance your career.

---

95   The apology was clear and to the point. Sitting and making eye contact shows sincerity. You gave background information to explain your reaction, not to justify it.
96   Your teen is not your therapist, but your disclosure is appreciated and your change in character has been noticed.
97   You wait to see if your teen follows your lead and takes responsibility as well.
98   Your modeling and silence worked. Maybe your teen felt guilty, but had he not apologized, you could easily have said, "Is there anything you want to take responsibility for?"
99   This will not be the last time you lose your cool or your teen doesn't clean up. The message is that you made the relationship the priority. The disagreement is not personal, and you now have a shared goal to work on.
100 The nonverbal gesture and comment tell you that things are now copacetic.
101 Not holding on means that you can both move on to other topics that bolster the relationship.

The Team Approach

Before addressing your teen on an important issue with another parent or caregiver, agree upon a focus and consequences (if necessary). Decide who will be in the lead role and have a plan B. Preparing beforehand promotes transparency and minimizes your child's ability to manipulate either caretaker or the outcome of the conversation.

The one not in the lead role monitors the discussion, watching for any breakdown in communication. If the observing parent notices the parent or child communicating in a way that detracts from the focus of the conversation, that parent can intervene. If the lead parent begins to lose control, the second parent can take over to keep the conversation moving forward or propose a break. A subtle gesture (scratching the head) can signal a switch off or temporarily time out.

This only works when the nonleading parent can stay calm when seeing the other parent lose her temper. Just as you can get entangled in your teen's emotions, parents can get caught up in each other's triggers or be triggered by the same stimulus. At least one parent needs to be in control at all times so that objectivity and rationality remain intact.

The lead parent usually becomes the object of focus, allowing the other to de-escalate or provide clarification. Switch lead roles regularly so that one is not always perceived as "the enforcer" and the other as "the cool parent." It is important that your child views both of you as supportive. When an interaction involves more than one caregiver, all need to be on the same page when raising issues and making critical points. Dissention allows your child to "split" you, seeking out the parent who is more likely to agree.

Support each other when making decisions or rules, even when you do not fully agree. This is not to say that parents shouldn't express a difference of opinions. Civil debate in front of your teen is a great opportunity to demonstrate that adults can have differing opinions and be respectful when discussing them. However, if you cannot reach an amicable agreement with your partner, continue the discussion privately. If your child does witness a dispute, be sure to make repairs with the other person as well as with your teen. Below is another example of an effective apology to your teen following such an event:

> *You: I'm sorry for raising my voice at Mom/Dad earlier when we were discussing your grades. My blowing up had nothing to do with you. We disagreed about some points. I need to know when to stop before my emotions get the best of me.*

This apology is important for three reasons. You make it clear that your teen had nothing to do with your heightened emotions; in other words, this is *your* issue. You model taking responsibility for losing self-control by making a repair, and it shows concern for your relationship with the other caretaker.

Use support from outside of the home. Enlist the help of other adults to reinforce what you wish to teach. For example, asking your teen's coach to talk to her about slipping grades can help bolster the message you wish to convey. It also shows your teen that other adults care about her overall well-being. Working with others allows you to debrief, seek other ideas, and discuss what worked and what did not. Be open minded when receiving feedback, and be mindful when giving advice to others.

What You Can Learn from How Your Teenager Ensures His Health and Wellness

You do not have to worry about your teen not looking after his health and wellness. Your teen will sleep if tired and eat if hungry. If he wants to have fun, he will find something entertaining to do. If your teen feels the need to belong, he will ask to go to a friend's house or invite someone over. Your teen may put health and wellness before school and work, whereas you may put work and school before your wellness. You will not always agree with the way your teen takes care of his wellness, but rest assured that it will not be neglected for long.

Between the demands of work and home, there are numerous reasons to put off doing things that promote your well-being. Find ways to satisfy work and wellness together, or do as your teen does and put your health and wellness first. Neglecting yourself for too long will negatively affect your ability to parent effectively and maintain a healthy relationship with your teen. How can you help your teen be well if you are not well yourself?

Your teenager is mainly trying to satisfy her needs and looking after her well-being. You may see this as selfish, but the behavior is by developmental design. Your teen is on the boundary between childhood and adulthood. From one day to the next, your teen will display attitudes and behaviors that promote one or the other. Your teen is busy exploring, playing, seeking inspiration, and inspiring others. Most of all, it is a time when critical connections to self and others are occurring. Much energy is needed in these transformative years, not leaving much time or energy to think of others.

As your teen learns from you to be considerate of others, you can learn from your teen to think more of yourself. This is not to say that you should neglect your family and job obligations, drain your bank account on an extravagant shopping spree, or escape to an exotic tropical island. Do think twice about the choices you make and how you respond to meeting your needs. How often do you consider your health and wellness? The next time you face a conflict between fulfilling your teen's needs and your own, do not be quick to sacrifice the latter. Is it a shared need? If so, find a common interest that satisfies the mutual need. It could turn into an activity you do with your teen well into the future.

Do you need to help your teen satisfy needs every time he asks? If your teen can take care of it alone or with the help of someone else, encourage it. If your help is needed, think of how you can benefit from the situation. You do not need to be a martyr in order to be a good parent. Your health and well-being are as important as your child's. Make sure that you get what you need to remain healthy by finding ways to care for yourself.

You can take tips from your teenager on how to promote wellness using what you discover in your own home. The next time you go into your child's room, look at how the room is set up. Look at the objects your teen has collected and has on display. Do not concern yourself with the orderliness of the room; just take in what you see as it relates to her well-being. Do not look at the room from the doorway; this is the parent perspective (looking from the outside in). Go into the room, sit on the bed or a chair, and observe from within. Move around the space, and pick things up. Put yourself in her shoes; see the space through her eyes.

What do you see? You might find any one of the following: pictures, drawings, clothing (both clean and dirty and some not belonging to your child), books, magazines, toys, school items, a musical instrument, jewelry, hygiene and beauty products, sports equipment, awards, trophies, pictures, posters, crumbs and wrappers, a television, a video game system, gadgets, and odd trinkets collecting dust. While overlooking the chaos, what can you learn about what your teen finds important? What have you learned about her that you did not know? How can you use this as a means to improve your own health and wellness?

When you view the organization of your teen's bedroom from a needs and values perspective, you will see what is high on her list of priorities. The space is made to promote her well-being. The clues you are seeing, touching, and smelling likely satisfy the needs of fun, freedom, belonging, and power. What need do you give most of your attention to? Most likely it is survival in the sense of providing for your family by paying for housing, utilities, food, clothing, transportation, health insurance, schooling, and so on. This is expected, but tend to the four other basic needs to promote a balanced lifestyle.

Looking around your child's room, you may see pictures of friends having fun. When was the last time you had fun with a friend? Maybe you see a trophy or an award for an academic or athletic achievement. When was the last time someone praised you for a job well done? Maybe you see a musical instrument on the floor and recall how you once played an instrument or always wanted to learn how to play one but never did. You might see a new pair of pants that you recently bought for your teen. When was the last time you bought an outfit for yourself?

Allocate more resources to creating environments that balance your needs and help you live a more fulfilling life. What values are being expressed by your teen that you have been neglecting? Which of those values could you incorporate into your life to improve your well-being? How can you add time and resources for creativity, humor, nutrition, friendships, or self-expression? Use the relationship chart in this lesson and the EPIC model to support neglected needs and values that enhance your wellness.

Lesson 7 Highlights

Care for Yourself and Your Home
- Incorporate regular mental, physical, emotional, and spiritual exercise into your family's needs and value system, and turn free time into health and wellness time.
- Ensure that spaces in your home support family values, and allow your teen to use the space he has to support his needs and lifestyle.

Staying Cool When You Are Feeling Hot
- Prepare yourself before a potentially emotional conversation by completing the preconversation questions and reviewing your communication toolbox.
- If you cannot reach an agreement or emotions are running high, remember your BATNA, end the discussion, and try again when you both are calm.

Learning from Mistakes
- Mistakes remain as such unless you turn them into opportunities to learn how to improve your decision-making skills and control your emotions.
- It is important to model an apology and make a repair when you make a mistake.

The Team Approach
- Work together and support each other on important matters and switch off leading roles when addressing issues.

- Ask others in your support network to help promote shared values.

What You Can Learn from How Your Teenager Ensures His Health and Wellness
- Pick up tips on how your teen uses spaces in your home to fulfill needs and promote values that contribute to her well-being.
- Just as your teen is taking initiative in fulfilling his needs, free up time and resources to look after your wellness.

Lesson 8:
Fear Not, Let Go, and Move On

Where fear is, happiness is not.

Seneca

You don't need strength to let go of something. What you really need is understanding.

Guy Finley

Life moves on and so should we.
Spencer Johnson, *Who Moved My Cheese?*

Looking Back Can Help the Relationship Move Forward

Long ago, you embarked on a journey of self-discovery, trying to make sense of the world and your place in it. You dealt with fitting in with peers, discovering hidden abilities, stumbling upon romance, and finding an answer to the question "Who am I, and what is my purpose?"

Have you become all that you are? You reach an age (coincidently when your child is between the teen and young adult years) when you would like to believe that you have it all figured out. It is easy to convince yourself that no further self-development is necessary. You can sit back and reap the rewards of your efforts and pass on your wisdom to your teenager.

Maybe you are comfortable with your job, partner, home, and friends. You have your retirement all planned out, but your soul is sending you signals of uneasiness, like the distressing sound of a mosquito buzzing around your head at night as you try to fall asleep. Though some friendships may no longer be as important as they once were, you still go out when you wish to seek out others. You continue finding excuses to not do what you always wanted to do. You ponder a new career path but still have the letter of resignation you wrote a year ago. Your relationship with your partner has lost some of its luster, and as much as you desire it to be more fulfilling, you accept it as normal.

    Why do these fleeting inquiries surface at this time in your life? As your teen is preparing to be launched into the world, the mirroring effect beckons you to run through your own checklist to see if you are ready for the next phase of your life and heading in the direction you want to go. Just as you were advised to ask your teenager open-ended questions, do the same with yourself. The quality of the question influences the quality of the response. Use the examples below as a guide to asking reflective questions that produce meaningful responses. The only thing to fear is not taking action. There are endless possibilities to explore, play, inspire others, be inspired, and connect with yourself and others.

Uninspiring questions	Inspiring questions
Is this all there is in life?	How can I make my life more fulfilling?
Why am I not a better parent?	How can I improve my parenting?
Why do I feel stuck in my job?	What can I do to make my career more interesting?
Am I happy with who I am?	What can I do to further grow?
Am I happy in my relationship?	How can I spice up my romance?

Remembering what it was like to be a teenager allows you to let go of your teen and will help you move on with your life. Recalling your own adolescence also gives you a treasure trove of stories to share with your child. As you recall your past, you are sure to be reminded of events that are eerily similar to ones that occurred or are currently going on with your teen.

Your teenage adventures and mishaps will captivate your teen's attention. Blunders from your adolescence probably did not irrevocably tarnish your family name or haunt you into adulthood. Most likely, the same will hold true for your teen. Use your judgment when recounting your past, taking into consideration your child's age and the appropriateness of your story. Share stories for the purpose of offering insight into a current situation or for connecting. Sharing does not mean that you excuse irresponsible behaviors, but stories about difficulties you encountered or invaluable lessons you learned in your teenage years can do the following:

- Ease your teen's worries (and your own) by normalizing the situation
- Improve your teen's understanding (and your own) of the situation
- Improve your teen's ability to solve problems and take in other perspectives
- Make you approachable (willing to relate similar experiences), empathetic (trying to see the situation from his perspective), and human (showing that you have flaws)

No matter how many times a lesson is taught through one of your stories, your teen will choose how to cope with life. Regardless of the outcome of your teen's decisions, it is important to respect her choices and, as importantly, to have your teen take ownership of the consequences of her actions. When things do not go the way you think they should have, look for what can be used as a learning opportunity. How many times does it take you, even now, to learn a lesson? What lessons are you still learning that originated in your adolescent years!

Sharing stories from your past levels the playing field and opens you up to questions. Your teen will appreciate this shift in dynamics, as he gets closer to adulthood. By sharing, you will be more mindful and less likely to judge or scold. The next time you do not approve of what your teen does, he can say, "How can you call me out, when you did the same thing as a teen?" Respecting such questions will make your limits more reasonable, and this will increase compliance. Rather than being hypocritical and authoritative, you will respond understandingly.

Give attention to the good times or funny moments when looking back at your teenage years. Minimize stories that condone irresponsible behaviors for the sake of humor or to impress your teen (unless you are using yourself as an example of what not to do). A funny story about you is sure to put a smile on your teen's face. Sharing past experiences will help foster your relationship and increase the likelihood of your teen opening up about what is happening in her life without having to pry. Making entertaining disclosures can lighten up a situation or shift the focus. Each time you or your teen shares a personal story, communication barriers break down and the lines of communication open, further solidifying your relationship.

Fear, Whether Real or Imagined, Is Important to Understand

Any stage of childhood development can give a parent reason to be fearful and anxious, but being overly concerned can hamper your teen's development and prevent your relationship from growing. Fear and anxiety increase when you are uncertain or do not know. As an infant, your child's crying possibly provoked anxiety because he could not tell you what was wrong. Now, even though your teen can tell you what the problem is, you may not be properly informed, and you are not always in his presence. Keep your fears in check to make it easier to emotionally let go and allow your teen to move on as a self-aware, confident young adult.

Your teen is beginning to: choose a career path, drive, sample with alcohol and drugs, become sexually active, work, associate with people you do not know or approve of, and explore the world unsupervised. You can sit anxiously at home, worrying about all that can go wrong, but does that benefit you or your child? Will it change any situation your child is in? Will your anxiety calm your teen or help her feel that you trust her?

Some degree of fear and anxiety is normal and is a means of self-preservation, but you do not want your child to be incapacitated by your distress. Excessive worrying increases the likelihood that your child will become what you do not want: distant, overly fearful, uncertain, and anxious. There are effective ways to cope with fears that do not entail hourly texts, home sobriety tests, and the like.

Instill trust. As you see less of what your teenager does, you must talk more. The quality of your communication depends on how safe your teen feels about being honest with you. Showing too much fear or always speaking from a fear-based perspective will undermine this process, and your teen will not want to share information for fear of your response. This will create an unhealthy and self-perpetuating cycle: the less your teen speaks or the more dishonest he becomes, the more fearful you will be. Furthermore, your anxiety will rise when your teen doesn't want to tell you about a problem out of fear of making the situation worse. How can you avoid this dynamic and keep your fears in check?

How is your child affected by how you cope with fear? Brainstorm what your anxieties are. Once you have identified a few, determine whether they are real or imagined. At any given time, a parent's worst fears can come true, but based on what you know about your child, is there reason to be gravely concerned about a matter as it affects your teen's safety, security, and future? If yes, consult with a professional.

Let's say you allowed your teen to go to the unsupervised party from Lesson 1, and you became anxious. Was it because the last time your teen returned from a party with no adult supervision she smelled of booze or told you that she had a drink or two? Did she return home past her curfew, high or drunk? If yes, some level of anxiety is reasonable, but does it mean you hit the panic button and place your child under house arrest? Recall your own unsupervised adolescent party experiences. If your teen is going to experiment, is it not better for it to occur while you can regularly talk about her ability to cope with high-risk situations and examine consequences of her decisions?

If this is the first time that you believe your teen is going to a party where alcohol and maybe drugs are present and you are concerned about how he will respond, what is the basis of your fear? In the end, there is only trust. Trust is tied to how connected you are to your child, how healthy and open your relationship is, and how high-risk situations were dealt with in the past. Your level of trust will determine your willingness to give your teen opportunities to prove that he can test limits and make responsible choices.

Check in with your teen. How does he feel or think about your concern? Your teen will be more likely to appreciate and accept your concerns if he knows you respect his opinion. What did he say about what went on at the party? How did he deal with peer pressure? Maybe marijuana was offered, and he declined. Maybe he tried it and didn't like it, or maybe he did. Experimentation will happen whether you know about it or not. By asking, you can discuss the ramifications and keep the dialogue open.

In addition to determining whether your fear is real or imagined, it is important to understand your fears, because, although unlikely, an incident can occur and may require your immediate attention. Not being prepared or being unaware of a fear can result in shock or inaction, or you could overreact and exacerbate the problem. If your child returns home intoxicated from a party, you might have a verbal altercation or an emotional outburst. You could also overreact irrationally (thinking that your child is an alcoholic the first time you smell alcohol on her breath). On the other hand, if an issue is deemed significant by an outside authority such as school personnel, or if a behavior is negatively impacting your teen's health or significantly interfering with her education, relationships or work, consult a professional.

Turn fear into a learning experience. Focus on what your teen gained from an unpleasant experience. Listen to his concerns, teach him coping skills, and provide support as he explores and grows. Most phases will pass with time. As the parent, you are home base—the foundation, the one to turn to in times of need. Your teen looks for you to be calm and able to handle the difficulties of adolescence when he needs a shoulder to lean on.

If you cannot help your teen, especially in times of need, why should your teen put energy into the relationship? Would you want a close relationship with someone who is not encouraging, who only looks at what can go wrong, who distrusts you, and who cannot help you in times of need? If your teen sees you having difficulty dealing with something that is not even happening to you, how confident should you expect your child to be in your ability to cope with the situation she is actually in? How will this attitude shape your child's self-worth? Express your confidence in both your ability to assist her and her ability to overcome challenges and difficult situations.

Letting Go for the Sake of Holding On

Accepting your child as a teenager and treating him accordingly will result in a newfound connection, one that is appropriate for a soon-to-be young adult. Thinking that your teen is still a child will only annoy your teen. It stunts your growth and his. Let go, and form a new physical and emotional attachment that is appropriate for where your teen is in life. You will be on a path to fostering the healthy relationship your teen desires and appreciates, and you free up energy for your own personal development.

You may no longer hold hands while walking, but you have not become obsolete. Just because you've redefined the relationship, do not underestimate your continued value and influence on your child. Ironically, by treating your teen like a young adult, you could see the physical closeness you once had return. Hugs and kisses may still sporadically occur, and when physical or verbal signs of affection spontaneously happen, be thankful—tell your teen how much you appreciate the gesture and that you enjoy being supportive.

Letting go means opening yourself up to scrutiny. As your teen enters the adolescent and young adult years, she will become a more informed and critical consumer. You will talk about more adult topics, and her concept of justice and morality will develop. She will begin taking on ideas outside your sphere of influence. Expect your beliefs, words, and actions—although still influential—to be more closely examined and questioned. View these debates as opportunities to embrace your teen as an individual, not as a loss of that cute little person who once listened to you and did everything you said.

Even through the difficult times—when you told your teen no—your teen will wake up in the morning, possibly still bitter but appreciative of your important role in her life. Your teen is sure to let go of your tough parenting moments as long as you show the ability to let go of past errors in judgment and the outdated image you might have of her. She will remain a loyal fan even after fierce arguments as long as you maintain an active role, remain connected, and provide unconditional love.

Letting go of your teen physically, mentally, and emotionally will allow you to turn to your own physical, mental, and emotional state. Fixating less on how you would like your teen to be allows you to think about how *you* would like to be. That can be a frightening place to arrive at, but it is more worrisome to think that there is nothing more for you to learn. Watching your teen grow can inspire you to take hold of your life and see what more you are capable of doing. What attitudes and behaviors can you take on that bring you closer to who you are?

Moving On with the End Goal in Mind

What are you trying to accomplish with your teen? The more appropriate question to ask is what your teen is trying to accomplish during these transformative years. If you haven't, ask him. What was the answer? Did he want to be valedictorian? Be proficient in three languages? Play two instruments? Develop talents in several sports? Graduate at the top of the class from an Ivy League university and work in a certain profession for the next forty years?

Are these the end goals? Is it not better to live responsibly, respectfully, contentedly, and purposefully? At the end of the day, does it matter that your teen didn't make the varsity team or the dean's list, wasn't accepted into the school you had hoped, or did not choose your preferred profession? Be happy if your teen has a direction, and support it. Your teen is trying to fulfill her desires, not make *your* dreams come true. Let your teen take care of her business, and you can take care of your own.

The purpose of letting go is to allow both of you to move toward the next phase of life. What does that look like for your teen? That answer may not exist yet. This question could be more pertinent for you. Maybe your job is steady and secure, but is it the right fit for you? Is it allowing you to give and grow? Are you able to perform to your potential?

The answers to these questions will surface. We all would like to know ahead of time what awaits us, but for most of us, life doesn't work that way. No one arrives at a point without having to travel there. You must be courageous enough, like your teen, to embark on the journey. Do not underestimate the learning that occurs along the way.

Having a framework that allows the process to unfold and get you closer to who you are is most important. The eight lessons presented in this book can help you with this process if you internalize the material, apply the techniques, and trust the process by allowing your teen's life and yours to unfold. This is not only a book on parenting teens. It is also a guide on living your life as you were meant to be. Self-actualization is a never-ending process.

You can get lost by not paying attention to your internal map, but there is always time to change the road you are on. We all carry an internal compass to guide us. Your teen is always looking at his compass, seeking, searching, and exploring. He may seem lost, because he is deciding which road to take, sometimes taking the scenic route or going off the trail and discovering uncharted territories. Encourage your teen to get lost in discovery, and follow his lead. Heed the call to change direction for the sake of learning, no matter how frightful it looks from the outside or how messy it feels from the inside.

You will never be able to completely prevent your teen from becoming who she is, and attempting to do so can come at the expense of the relationship. You cannot suppress your nature for too long without a consequence. Join your teen on her journey, and be open to taking one yourself. Move on. Go instinctually with what you desire to do and see where it takes you.

If your child's ambitions seem farfetched, do not put him down for having outlandish thoughts. Even the most unusual of aspirations has elements that can be encouraged. If your teen wishes to become a professional athlete, do not be quick shatter that dream. Are the chances slim? Possibly, but that is not the point. You have a place from which you can start. See what benefits can be extracted and championed. What qualities do professional athletes possess? Think about the importance of training, nutrition, physical fitness, discipline, dedication, learning, and resiliency in handling disappointments. Is there anything on this list that you would discourage your child from learning, regardless of the path he chooses? Your child will realize his chances of making a living in professional sports (or any other profession he chooses). Do you think all professional athletes had the full support of their parents?

Let life be your child's lesson, because you have no idea what will become of your teen. This is up to her to figure out. In the meantime, support your child's development, and instill the values that will help her be successful as a person, regardless of what she becomes.

Your teen requires guidance, and so do you. You are not clueless and neither is your teen. Avoid the trap of perceiving your teen as always needing redirection. Your lack of confidence in his ability to maintain order will result in you dictating what needs to be done. The more you influence decisions, the less confident he will become, and in the end, your fears will become an unwanted reality. Give your child opportunities to prove his worth. That is true empowerment.

This lesson requires you to think on a larger scale, to look at the big picture, and to decide what matters. All this talk about adolescence could have you digging deep within and reconnecting with your own youthful spirit. As your teenager moves from adolescence to adulthood, you can hold on to the past that is slipping through your fingers and be left out of the transformational process, or you can release your grip on what no longer exists, open up your heart and hand, and join your teen on her journey right now.

What You Can Learn from How Your Teenager Doesn't Fear, Lets Go, and Moves On

Having worked for many years with disadvantaged youth and having adolescents of my own, my respect, appreciation, and admiration of adolescents has grown tremendously. They all had to overcome their fears, let go of the past, and move on to cope with the present reality. Their here-and-now mentality did not allow the past to interfere with the present for long.

There is much to learn from watching your child transition to adolescence and young adulthood. Spend as much time taking notes and picking up tips from your teen as you do giving counsel. He has fears, but he is more likely than you to face those fears, overcome those anxieties, and take a risk. As a natural risk taker, he is inquisitive, adventurous, and open to new experiences. For him, fear only delays an action, whereas for you it can cause long-term paralysis.

With encouragement and support, your teen can overcome most any obstacle, and so can you.

If you allow it, your fears can keep you in a state of suspended animation. Maintaining the status quo in spite of an urge from within to make a change feels safe, but this is a false sense of security. You want to explore a new desire but fear the disruption it may cause to your relationships, finances, reputation, or family routine. It could be as simple as starting a new hobby, or more life changing, such as switching careers, leaving a long-term relationship, or moving out of state or to another country. In all cases, fear can become an excuse for inaction.

The ability to act in the face of fear improves the more it is practiced and encouraged. Just as your teen uses you as a support to overcome challenges, you can gain backing from your teen. When I was contemplating whether to write this book, I asked my oldest son what he thought. He said, "Dad, just do it! Go ahead. Why not?" He made it sound simple while I was questioning my ability and fearing the unknown. With a few simple words of encouragement from my son, my concerns disappeared.

Approach anxiety the way your teenager does. Your teen's curiosity and desire for reward override fears about crossing lines and playing with boundaries. Take a chance, make a new experience, seek out support, and act on a gut instinct. All these lead to new opportunities. If you are hesitating about making a life change or struggling with a decision, ask yourself what your teen would do. Even better, ask her for tips on how to move forward.

Letting go of you is one of your teen's goals, and it should be one of yours as well. Rather than lamenting it as a loss, rejoice in knowing that you helped your teen reach this developmental milestone. Letting go means saying goodbye, which is one of the most important words you will utter. The more often you can say it in earnest and appreciate what it means, the more you will appreciate the interactions you have with your teen.

Learn from the way your teenager gradually lets go of you, because it allows him to develop relationships with others. Let go of old dynamics that no longer apply to your relationship; this frees up time to make new connections and experiences. Become curious and excited (like your teen) about what you can now allow into your life. Your teen is looking forward to all the possibilities that are waiting. You can too.

In the summer of 2011, my wife and I decided that she and our sons would live for a year in Austria, my wife's country of origin that she had left in 1998. We had always talked about trying to make a life in Austria. We saw the decision to significantly disrupt our comfortable, routine lifestyle as a learning opportunity for the family.

It was the first time we lived separately, and we saw each other only once every several months. Additionally, my family was living with my wife's parents when, several months after their arrival, my father-in-law was diagnosed with terminal brain cancer and died six months later. Because I could not be with my sons on a consistent basis, I was counting on him to assist in a paternal role. In all, my sons dealt with being separated from their father, living in a different culture, watching their grandfather die, attending school in German, and leaving old friends with the challenges of making new ones.

When I think of all that my boys endured during this period of letting go of all that was familiar, I am amazed by how they managed personally, socially, and academically. They had to confront numerous fears and let go of what was known, and they did so by living in the moment. Not being able to move on will result in reverting back to what you are trying to let go of and holding onto thoughts and behaviors that no longer apply.

My boys moved on by living their lives, going to school, assimilating, and learning about themselves in a new environment. When I needed the strength to remain in the here and now, I thought about all that they were dealing with at a young and impressionable age. Along with the hundreds of youth I had worked with, they inspired me, gave me the strength to deal with life's uncertainties, and gave me the courage to let go of realities that no longer applied. They allowed me to see what life had to offer by giving up my job, home, friends, parents, and country.

I have determined that the key to adolescent resiliency is the ability to face fears, let go of what no longer works, and find people, things, and ideas that aid development and growth. To help move on, I focused on writing this book. Writing helped overcome my fear of disconnecting from my family, and it helped me let go of the family life we had in Massachusetts.

My basic needs never subsided, and the prolonged separation prevented me from satisfactorily fulfilling them. My core values sustained me and those I adopted from my children helped me take the steps necessary to manage my fears, let go of a reality that no longer fit, and make the most significant changes in my life. The EPIC model guided me as I watched how my children were successfully using it to make their transition. The rules I put in place to provide structure allowed me to achieve short-term goals. I occasionally made small gestures to recognize the changes I was making.

As adults, we can be stuck in the past, paralyzed by the present, or fixated on the future. When we feel our gut telling us something, we tend to override our instincts with our intellect or allow ourselves to become overwhelmed with emotion. Adolescents are better at staying in the here and now, listening to their instincts, and staying true to their nature. This approach leads to action that is in line with who you are. There is not too much of a past for them to get lost in, and the future is too far away to be a concern.

Think of a difficult situation or a troubling period your child was in and how her ability to overcome resulted from staying in the moment and trusting her gut reaction. These were probably moments when your teen's actions involved overcoming a fear, letting go, and moving on. Use your teen's triumphs as motivation to deal with an obstacle that is currently in your way.

Your teen can rise to the occasion and overcome seemingly insurmountable obstacles. Appreciate the youthful spirit, even if it manifests in moodiness and defiance, because these are the by-products of a relentless and yearning attitude, one that does not easily surrender. Your teenager is a treasure trove of inspiration. Embrace your determined, creative, and resilient teen as someone from whom you can learn to become the parent and person you are. Doing so will create a win-win-win scenario in which you, your child, and your relationship all benefit.

Lesson 8 Highlights

Looking Back Can Help the Relationship Move Forward
- Telling stories from your own teenage years can ease fears, promote understanding, strengthen your relationship, and help your teen to reframe and resolve problems.
- Personal disclosures should be appropriate and applicable to your teen's situation.

Fear, Whether Real or Imagined, is Important to Understand
- Trust your teen's judgment and abilities. Excessive fear will diminish self-confidence and turn your teen away from you, creating a cycle of distance and worry.
- Knowing your fears allows you to better respond when they do arise, making your teen more likely to come to you in times of need.

Letting Go for the Sake of Holding On
- Letting go of your teen physically, mentally, and emotionally will allow you to pay attention to your physical, mental, and emotional growth.
- Your teen will verbally and physically show her appreciation to you for being treated for who she is and not how you want her to be.

Moving On with the End Goal in Mind
- Make the end goal a process that supports your teen's development, not an outcome that satisfies your desires.
- Allowing your teen to move on will allow you to move on with your life, using your teen as a model for how to seize the moment and accomplish your goals.

What You Can Learn from How Your Teenager Fears Not, Lets Go, and Moves On
- Your teen will provide a model for how to overcome fears, inspiring you and giving you the confidence to deal with your own challenges.
- Letting go and moving on allows you to remain connected and helpful to your teen. You will also have more time and resources for your own personal development.

Conclusion

The pomegranate fruit contains an enormous amount of seeds, symbolizing fertility, prosperity, abundance, and generosity.[102]

The Conflict Over Pomegranate Juice

When we were living apart, my wife, Susanne, one day told me that our fourteen year old had called her because he and his eleven-year-old brother were fighting over pomegranate juice. You read correctly—pomegranate juice. If you have had the pleasure of removing the seed casings from a pomegranate, you know it is a tedious task. My younger son had just made fresh juice when his brother came into the kitchen, wanting some. After all the hard work, he was not keen on sharing.

Susanne said that she usually did not respond coolly to such matters, but this time was different. Instead of passing judgment and lecturing, she was patient and tried to understand the root of the conflict. Disputes over minor issues happen frequently when there is more than one child, and these are valuable opportunities to help your children resolve a conflict regardless of how petty it appears to be. Spend less time judging and more time coaching.

---

102 Joseph Panek, "The Pomegranate—Symbol and Myth," http://www.aseekersthoughts.com/2009/12/pomegranate-symbol-and-myth.html.

Knowing there was something deeper going on that pertained neither to pomegranate juice nor to her, she knew that adding her emotions to the mix would have shifted the focus off the issues between the boys. Becoming the third irate person only mirrors your children's emotional response and condones the behavior you wish to stop.

If you become too emotionally involved, quarreling siblings will drop their issue to align against you. This adds another issue while the original problem remains unresolved. You will never eliminate disputes so use these opportunities to improve your teen's ability to resolve conflict by not allowing your opinion (or anger) to get in the way. Remember that it is not about you—and the issue most likely is not what the quarrel is about.

As a parent and former manager of a group home for youth in conflict with the law, I learned that there is usually more going on beneath the surface when a fight or argument occurred over seemingly petty things. Applying the relationship chart from Lesson 5 can help find the root causes of conflicts and the motives of those involved. Below is the chart as it applies to this dispute. Drinking relates to survival and this need brought them together in the kitchen. The need for power (in the absence of belonging) caused the conflict.

	Younger child	**Older child**
Need #1: Survival	Wanted something to drink	Wanted something to drink
Need #2: Belonging	Wanted to be recognized and appreciated as a sibling	Wanted to be recognized and appreciated as a sibling
Need #3: Power	Wanted acknowledgment of his work	Wanted respect for being the big brother
Values	Achievement, independence, recognition, and politeness	Craftiness, ease, and seniority
Basic rules	Acknowledge and respect what others do, and ask before taking	See what you can get away with, let others do the work for you, and use your status to get what you want
Small gestures	All gestures were self-serving and not for the sake of the relationship (belonging)	All gestures were self-serving and not for the sake of the relationship (belonging)

When resolving conflicts, no matter how our values, rules, and gestures differ, we all share the same needs. Whenever two or more people are with one another, the need for belonging is imperative in creating a peaceful environment. Look at the words most often used when entering and leaving another person's space (and learned when traveling abroad): *hello, goodbye, excuse me, sorry,* and *thank you.* These words show acknowledgment and respect. It is not a coincidence that according to the Guinness World Record as of 2009, the United Nations General Assembly's Universal Declaration of Human Rights—a six-page text written in response to the atrocities of World War II—holds the record as the most translated document in the world, with 370 translations. The thirty articles that comprise this landmark document preserve, respect, and acknowledge the need for belonging for all humankind.

Fulfilling the need to belong when you enter a space occupied by someone else does not have to be verbal or overtly nonverbal. If nothing else, wait and allow the other person to fulfill his need for being there without judgment or interference. You can offer your assistance, acknowledging your need to belong and if it is accepted, then you also fulfill the need of power. As soon as the older brother entered the kitchen, irrespective of what both boys were doing, the need for belonging kicked in for both of them, but neither acknowledged this shared need through values, rules, or gestures.

Conflict arises when we lose sight of the needs that bind us (in this case, survival, power, and belonging) and focus on the values, rules, and gestures that make us distinct. My younger son felt that he alone should have been entitled to drink the juice. The value of sharing was high for the older brother, because he would have been on the receiving end. The younger one could have offered a cup of juice, but sharing was vaguely on the mind of the younger brother, because he would have been on the giving end.

The older brother did not practice a value that the younger appreciated: politeness. He did not ask if he could have some juice; he just moseyed into the kitchen, expecting it. He falsely believed that his senior status entitled him to have his wish, regardless of his younger brother's intention. He disregarded the basic rules of asking for permission and acknowledging his brother's efforts. Both disregarded kind gestures of any sort.

It becomes evident that the differing values, rules, and gestures around seeding and juicing a pomegranate caused the conflict, not the pomegranate itself. This realization allowed my wife to look past the pomegranate and understand what the fuss was about. To help the boys process the incident, she acknowledged the needs they were trying to fulfill: thirst (survival), recognition (power), and their relationship as brothers occupying the same space (belonging). Starting by acknowledging what is shared is helpful in bringing people together, because it is common ground.

As differing values, rules, and gestures were discussed, Susanne acknowledged all that were displayed and had them come up with alternatives to more appropriately address their shared needs. They were told that their relationship as brothers was their BATNA and should supersede any argument over differing values, rules, and gestures. Emphasizing this point stressed the value of family as well as forgiveness.

Ironically, the young men with whom I worked, whose offenses violated societal values and rules, were quick to call staff members out on matters of noncompliance with established house values or rules. Their efforts to maintain civility showed me how they appreciated and respected a framework for living as long as it was consistently and fairly applied to all.

Your family will share similar values, rules, and gestures that show unity, respect, and appreciation. Each of you will also have differing ones requiring all to be respected and appreciated. My sons often remind me of house values, rules, and gestures, as well as those that make up who they are as individuals, and I appreciate it every time they do.

Made in the USA
Charleston, SC
07 January 2015